LUCAS CARLSON

FINDING
SUCCESS
IN FAILURE

True Confessions from 10 Years of Startup Mistakes

CRAFTSMAN
FOUNDER
Startups and Entrepreneurship

Give feedback on the book at: lucascarlson.net
Subscribe to the mailing list for extras and new
book releases at: findingsuccessinfailure.com

FINDING SUCCESS IN FAILURE:
True Confessions from Ten Years of Startup Mistakes

ISBN   978-0-9960452-3-0   *Hardcover*

        978-0-9960452-2-3   *Paperback*

        978-0-9960452-1-6   *Ebook*

To the three generations of women in my life:

Ema, Yoscelina, and Valentina...

Your support is all the success I will ever need.

Acknowledgements

Many people have asked me why I decided to write this book. I've been blessed by the support of amazing mentors all my life. I hope to repay them for all they have given me, and this book is an attempt to pay it forward. The worst thing I could imagine is for all the good advice I have been given to stop with me, so I will try to distill the best of it down for you.

This journey started out as a small blog and a podcast. The wonderful people who have been following along have been such an inspiration and their emails and messages mean the world to me. They are hugely responsible for the outcome of this book. They helped pick the title, the cover, and reviewed every chapter to keep me honest in giving the best advice I could.

If you would like to join along in the adventure, I'd love to hear from you and tell you about new thoughts, books, interviews an happenings in my life. Please join the mailing list at **findingsuccessinfailure.com** or send me a message directly at **lucascarlson.net** and let's make this a journey of entrepreneurship we take together.

Special thanks specifically go out to Ema, Roger, Justin, Tom, Richard, Surj, John, Chris, Jonas, Patrick, David, Rohit, Joe, Simon, Dave, Jonathan, Neil, Zach, Andrew, Frank, Tim, Rob and of course Yoscelina for the wisdom you have given me over the years. Thanks also to Eliot, Justin, Randy, Ryan, Ed, Kurt, Jeff, Sanjay, Thuy, Karl, Brandon, Oliver, Daniel, Tai and the hundreds of others who gave me incredible constructive feedback on this book. Finally, this book would not have been possible without Tucker Max, Zach Obront, Ann Maynard, Erin Tyler, Ian Claudius and all the folks at Book in a Box. Thank you all so much and I hope you enjoy the fruits of our labor.

Contents

Introduction

"*In expert tennis, 80% of the points are won, while in amateur tennis, 80% are lost. The same is true for wrestling, chess, and investing: Beginners should focus on avoiding mistakes, experts on making great moves.*"

— ERIK FALKENSTEIN

I felt like I was about to throw up as I uttered words I'd never thought I would have to: "I'm sorry, this is really hard, I appreciate everything you've done for me, but I have to let you go."

He looked at me stunned like a deer in the headlights. Though he knew things weren't going great recently, it looked like he hadn't even thought of being fired. He said: "Ok, wow. Didn't see that coming. So two weeks then?"

I had consulted my investors and lawyers the week before this conversation and they both told me that the termination should take effect immediately at the end of the day on a Friday. This was brutal. I said: "No, you will need to take your belongings home right now. Today was your last day."

A year earlier, when I started my first venture-backed company and hired my first employee, I was on cloud nine. Sitting in a coffee shop with this brilliant, talented programmer building my ideas, I thought to myself, *Finally after all these years, I've made it. I am a real entrepreneur.* Little did I know how much the real work of entrepreneurship was ahead of me. Like firing him.

Without my first programmer, I would have never been able to get the company off the ground. But as we grew from a team of two to six and twelve and twenty, the day came when the culture had shifted and we weren't working from coffee shops and living rooms anymore. We had our own office space.

I learned the hard way that sometimes the people you need in one size of an organization don't always fit as things grow. And though I couldn't have started without him, it was time that my first hire became my first fire.

The idea terrified me for weeks. I felt like I had failed my employee, even though we had tried multiple times to make it work. Every time I talked to my advisors, they would tell me: "Hire slow, fire fast." Or "Do it now, don't wait another day." But how could I be so cold to a friend who helped me get my company off the ground? What would I tell him? How would he react?

I hated myself. My heart was on the floor and my stomach was in my throat. I couldn't believe the things I said. I sounded like a total douche. What was I doing? How did things get so bad? Why was I even starting this company in the first place? This was not the last time I would have to do this, though. Not by a long shot.

I'm no Steve Jobs. I've spent years looking up to visionaries who've put a dent in the universe: Richard Branson, Mark Cuban, Elon Musk. These guys seem to get it. They seem to have some natural talent for building great companies almost instinctively.

But I'm not them. It's not wild success like theirs that has qualified me to write this book. My own successes have been wonderful, but much more modest. What qualifies me is that I've made every mistake an entrepreneur can make. Twice.

I spent a decade chasing short-term gains, quick money, and early exits. I chalked up my daily frustrations—with myself and with my companies—to the rigors of entrepreneurial life and I continued to grind through it. I wore down. I burned out. I tasted bankruptcy. And ultimately I came out on the other side with a very different perspective.

Nassim Taleb in his ground-breaking book *Antifragile* explains, "Negative knowledge (what is wrong, what does not work) is more robust to error than positive knowledge (what is right, what works)." Said another way, what worked for Richard Branson or Steve Jobs may or may not work for you, it's hard to tell. But it's very likely that what doesn't work for any entrepreneur won't work for you either. This is a book unlike other entrepreneurial books. Instead of telling you what to do, I try to tell you what not to do. I've tried to compose as many of my failures and the repeated failures I have seen from many entrepreneurs I have advised over the years as possible. I hope to teach you what doesn't work to help you minimize your downside as an entrepreneur so that you can stay in the game long enough to realize the unlimited potential upside.

With all my failures, I eventually realized that the only way I could ever build a company and a career that I was truly proud of was by treating startups as a long-term craft—by protecting the downside and exploiting upside optionality when it came. I became a craftsman founder dedicated to skillfully building companies that held a clear mission and honored my core values, a storyteller committed to building and maintaining relationships with customers, investors, and my personal support system. I devoted myself to creating, refining, and improving my craft for the long term. I learned to see the world in a different way by asking better questions.

"Quality questions create a quality life. Successful people ask better questions, and as a result, they get better answers."

— TONY ROBBINS

My life changed dramatically after repeatedly asking myself one simple question: *why?* Let's explore how. If you are like me, you started working at a startup because you hope to found a startup of your own one day. But how often have you stopped to ask yourself *why you are doing this?*

This question has bothered me since I was a small child. One Sunday, coming home from church, I was sitting in the back seat of our minivan and I asked my mom: "Why are we here?"

Of course she immediately thought, *Uh oh, isn't he a little young to be asking that?* She tried awkwardly to skirt around the question of the birds and the bees, but I said, *"No, Mom, why are we here? What's it for?"* She realized, with relief, that I was trying to ask what the meaning of life was but didn't have the words for it yet. I clearly remember a sensation of deep dread that morning. I think it was the first time I had ever felt dread.

But the meaning of life is not what I want to talk to you

about. Let's just focus on startups. *Why work at startups? Or why start a company?*

It doesn't matter if you are running a food cart, starting a law firm, or founding a high-tech company. It doesn't even matter if you are rich from having already sold companies, or if you are still living paycheck to paycheck. If you haven't put in the time to explore why you do the things you do, you might be pursuing the wrong things for the wrong reasons.

The trick is to go deeper than the shallow 'why.' Look closer at what most people are afraid to face: the *underlying* why of your motivation to work harder than anyone else you know.

The ultimate question is: What's that damn chip on your shoulder that you can't seem to get rid of?

The easy answer to the why question is: money. It's the wrong answer, of course; it's only surface level. But as a first-order approximation, it gives us a good starting point.

For years I thought money was my main motivation too. Sure, I wanted to change the world for the better, use the money to have more control over my life, and spend more time with my family.

But if I am honest with you, truly brutally honest... I really wanted to get rich. Badly. Embarrassingly so. I still do. I often dream of getting 'Uncle Scrooge rich,' right down to the swimming pool full of gold coins.

That would be amazing, albeit hard to swim in.

So, why didn't I just start a company early in my career? Everyone knows entrepreneurship can be a fast path to wealth. So why, like many people, did I begin my entrepreneurial journey by working at someone else's startup?

I was too scared to start my own company because I thought I didn't know enough to succeed. So, I got a job at a startup, hoping to learn its secrets while still getting a regular paycheck.

But here's the biggest takeaway from my time working in other people's startups: you won't get rich unless you are near the top of the pyramid.

It's an incredibly rare startup that makes its employees (who often own a fraction of a percent in company's stock) millionaires. Facebook and Twitter are the unicorns of startups, and if you are working for a startup with a fraction of a percent in equity, you are almost certainly not getting any closer to wealth than if you were working at any other regular job. Founders and executives can make out well with a small exit, but the employees rarely do better than buying a new car or maybe a small house.

There are still plenty of other great reasons to work for startups. You can wear multiple hats and deal with less (or at least different) politics. These are all valid motivations to work for startups, but getting fabulously wealthy is not a good reason to be a startup employee. After working as a startup employee for seven years, I realized that I was no closer to my goal of great wealth than when I started.

So I quit my job and started my own company. My new goal was to change the world for the better. And if I eventually got rich in the process, that wouldn't be bad either.

Many founders want to change the world for the better, and I ask them the same question I had to ask myself: *why?* Why do you want to change the world for the better? It certainly sounds more honorable and virtuous than admitting to pure greed, but it still doesn't address the deeper 'why.'

Over the years, I have advised and mentored hundreds of entrepreneurs, and I have heard every reason in the book for starting companies. Maybe you too want to make a difference. Or you want to create a legacy. Or you want to help technology reach new and exciting heights. Or you have a deep desire to help people around the world. Or, with the accumulated wealth, you want to give back to those around you.

Good, now we are at the second-order approximation. You want to change the world with your work, or you want to earn enough money to achieve some life-long noble aspiration.

Keep digging.

On the journey to discover why you really start companies, you'll have many false starts. My initial goal was to have so much money that I could do whatever I wanted, whenever I wanted. If I wanted to spend a year in Paris with my wife, I could. If I wanted to study the ancient game of Go in Japan while eating great ramen, I could. If I wanted to climb Mount Kilimanjaro, I could.

It took a long time for me to realize that this goal was actually a false choice. There was nothing to stop me from going on those adventures without having a lot of money. In fact, I had friends who have accomplished most of the things on my list without being rich. They slept in hostels and ate top ramen, but they made it work. Their examples were just one clue that the dream I created for myself wasn't my real motivation.

If you want to make money or change the world, you might think you want it in order to achieve some end goal. But I am telling you that any external goal you set for yourself is like the spoon in 'The Matrix'—it's just an illusion.

It might be a comforting illusion to think you have a noble reason for wanting to get rich, but that comfort keeps you from digging deeper. It's just like climbing a mountain: the higher you go, the harder it gets. There is no spoon. Why did I want the freedom I thought money could buy? Why did I want to improve things for programmers around the world? If you look past the illusion of those goals, what is left?

The proverbial chip on your shoulder.

Things were going great at the company I started, and it seemed like I could do no wrong. I felt it was finally my turn. At least for a while. After all, I had raised ten million dollars from great venture capitalists, I had hired over forty employees, and we had signed up over a hundred thousand developers for the service. If you believe the statistics you read in the news, my company was in the top 0.001% of businesses in America (at least when it comes to getting outside investment).

That was until revenue growth didn't meet investors' expectations. I had to lay off employees, and I didn't know if the service would stay open much longer. Firing my first employee those years earlier now looked like a walk in the park. In those difficult moments, I thought a lot about my goals in life. I examined my reasons for wanting to achieve personal freedom and to change the world for the better.

I had been working like a maniac, running my company, with no personal freedom at all. I had created a service that developers depended on. Now, I was facing a possible shutdown and pissing off a hundred thousand people. For what? Riches I might never get? To start all over again with another company? *Why?*

I had to peel another layer of the onion away in order to find the next answer. *I did startups because I had to.* I had a deep burning desire. I had been entrepreneurial since I was a kid, trying to sell dream catchers I made as a craft or when I wrote a book of magic tricks for Hoyle before I was old enough to legally sign a contract. It was in my blood. But I still couldn't pinpoint exactly why I had this burning desire yet.

If you're still keeping score, I had arrived at a third-order approximation. Getting here had taken years of introspection and I was finally getting close. But to make the real breakthrough, I had to ask myself one more time: *why?*

Why did I have to do startups? What did I have to prove?

Many great entrepreneurs share a secret they rarely talk about: a feeling of never being good enough. Of course, there are the Richard Bransons of the world, who claim perfectly happy childhoods, but many founders I know hide skeletons in their closet.

I will share with you one of my skeletons in hopes that it might help you discover your own. Maybe for someone out there, this story can act as a guidepost for thinking about your own motivations in a new light. The hard truth is that the skeletons don't stop chasing you just because you have more money.

When I was in middle school, my parents divorced. The divorce, however, didn't cause me any psychological distress. My father had already been away from the house a lot, so I was used to his absence. My father's absence caused me little distress.

In fact, in many ways I had a very happy childhood. After my parents' divorce, my mom overcompensated with love and generosity. She took us on regular vacations and took us to new countries and cool places almost every year. At Easter, my brother and I looked forward to large inflatable bunnies as big as us, surrounded with every chocolate known to man. At Christmas, the tree was always overflowing. Looking back now with two kids of my own, I have no idea how my mom was able to always provide so much on a meager teacher's salary.

But for my mom, life did become harder after the divorce. She suffered from health complications, depression, and a series of car accidents. She began turning to alcohol. When I confronted her about how much she drank, she would tell me that it was her only real friend.

Sometimes I would walk around the house and find a half-dozen glasses of half-finished white wine and know what was coming next. I would run to my younger brother's room and urge him to just try to go along with whatever Mom said. Accept the blame, don't fight it.

Alcohol-induced rages became a regular occurrence for a period of time. It was very scary and confusing for me as a child. I tried to protect my brother from them as best I could even though I barely had the tools to protect myself. To this day, my brother doesn't believe my mom had a serious problem with alcohol, which makes me both proud and sad.

I deeply love my mother, and she has since become sober, which has allowed me to create a new relationship with her. But in my youth, I often felt lost and out of control. I felt trapped in a scary and unpredictable world.

At the time, I thought my mom's rages were my fault. I thought that if I could just be a better son... if I could just get along better with my brother... if I was good enough, maybe my mom wouldn't have to drink so much.

But what does any of this have to do with starting companies? Digging into my past revealed a deeper motivation behind my drive to create startups.

I start companies to prove to myself that I am good

enough. I start companies with the hope that it will help me feel more whole inside—that I am worthy. I want to feel like I have the tools to control an unpredictable world. Almost as importantly, I want to pass on these tools to others, like I tried to do with my brother so many years ago. I hope to pass these tools on to you.

I write this book as a journal of lessons learned for my younger self. Notes on things that worked for me, and more especially notes on the endless combinations of things that didn't. I write this for those who need to move from "I want to start a company," to "I have started a company," but don't feel they have the tools yet.

This book will talk about the inner psychology of founding a startup. Though we will cover some logistics along the way, I want to walk you through how I learned to manage my own mind throughout the ups and downs of building a company. And, of course, I hope you will start or continue your own journey to discover your *why*.

This book is a compilation of things I wish someone had told me when I was starting my journey. It's the advice that I wish I'd received while I was spending all of my effort, energy, and time chasing short-term opportunities. It is the reoriented perspective that took me a decade to discover. It's the book I will re-read over and over again to keep reminding myself of these hard-earned lessons.

Entrepreneurship isn't about monetary wealth. Entrepreneurship is about the wealth you find within yourself when you succeed at achieving impossible goals and the growth you find when you fail. Entrepreneurship is about the relationships you build with yourself and those around you.

It can be incredibly transformative to found a company.

The process requires a level of self-examination that most of us fear. But it is more than worth it. And it's entirely in your control.

Your past can either cripple you or empower you. You choose. You can let your feelings of inadequacy, guilt, and shame keep you working jobs that suck your soul. Or you can go out and, with a little luck and guidance, write a new story of your life. It can be post-traumatic stress or it can be post-traumatic growth that defines you.

You know as well as I do that in reality you don't have a choice. Your skeletons chase you no matter where you hide. It's about time to find your inner strength to pull through and make something of yourself.

After laying off staff and regrouping, my company rallied with gusto. In the upswing, we were bought by a Fortune 150 company. It was not an inevitable outcome. It could have all easily fallen apart, and for many in the same position it does. But total failure would have been fine, because either way I still have work to do.

I still have a chip on my shoulder and a burning desire to help others through my work.

That's what entrepreneurship means to me. And that's what success means to me. Feeling good enough. Feeling worthy.

So do I feel good enough now? Do I feel worthy? Some days yes, some days no. But that's okay. It's a work in progress.

And it's the work of a lifetime.

Picking Startup Ideas

How do you come up with a great idea that adds real value to the world? Better yet, how do you recognize that idea from all the terrible ideas that sound like great ones?

Whenever I have an idea that I want to turn into a company, my first instinct is to go out and conquer it. I want to take action! I wake up in the morning and shove my wife. "Honey, listen to this. I've got a great idea." If I had a dime for every time I have told her that... Wait, that's an interesting startup idea. "Honey!"

However, I have come to learn that the worst thing I can do as an entrepreneur is to marry the first ideas that pop in my head. Why?

Because no matter what that idea is, after letting it sit for a day or two, the novelty often wears off and reality sets in. Many times I have refused to believe this. I get a high every time I come up with an idea that I think is brilliant. In the past, this high would lead to building the idea before testing the validity of it. I'd put in weeks or months of effort, or sometimes tens of thousands of dollars only to discover how bad the idea was when nobody wanted what I built.

It took years before I understood deeply the concept that that picking the right startup idea will almost always take up-front iteration, testing, and brutally honest assessments. The sooner I accepted that finding my best ideas was a process, not an event, the better off I was.

Think of it in terms of dating: you wouldn't marry someone immediately after a great first date. You'd spend time getting to know each other, seeing if your values and personalities are aligned, and making sure there weren't any obvious flaws that might destroy your relationship.

When it comes to startup ideas, it's best to play the field for as long as possible. As a founder, the smartest thing you can do is date other ideas before settling down. When I finally found my great idea, there was no doubt. It hit me like a ton of bricks. When things finally clicked, it was unlike anything I had ever experienced before. No longer was I begging and scratching for attention. Now people were clamoring to get access to my idea. I hadn't even built it yet: it was just a landing page, but people couldn't stop talking about it. And this went on for weeks and months, not just days.

I found myself with thousands of people on a waiting list, but I couldn't let thousands of people into a system that wasn't ready for it. To figure out who I would let in first, I created a form full of dozens of questions that I thought nobody in their right mind would spend their valuable time filling out. I thought it would take hours. Half of the people on my waiting list ended up filling out the survey with detailed information. This was like striking startup gold—it was exactly what I needed to know in order to build an even better product.

Finding the right idea takes time. But when you know, *you*

know beyond a shadow of a doubt. You may have doubts about whether you can pull it off, but you have no doubts that this idea is the one. Even if you are unfamiliar with this sensation, you must have faith that you will know it when it happens to you too. Until it happens, you must iterate through ideas ruthlessly. You must preserve your optionality for doubling down on a bigger opportunity.

This doesn't mean throwing out any idea that you have doubts about. Rather use it as a starting point for iteration. Date the idea, but keep playing the field. Let me tell you a story of a company which did exactly that.

There was once a decent little mobile startup called Burbn. It raised five hundred thousand dollars from top venture capitalists. But after a year of decent growth, they questioned whether things were growing as quickly as they hoped. They noticed when looking through stats that the most popular feature of their system by far was the photo sharing part. They made a tough call and built an entirely new app that focused exclusively on the photo sharing feature and called it 'Instagram.' Famously, they were acquired by Facebook for nearly one billion dollars just eighteen months later.

Many people don't find their biggest ideas until years into running their startup. But to find these big ideas you need to be looking for them. You can't be deceiving yourself by continuously looking at the positive and ignoring the negative. It's incredibly easy to have thirty percent month-over-month growth when you only have three users.

If you haven't yet started your business or quit your day job, even better. You can't deceive yourself with false traction, because you don't have any traction yet. Once you start a company and have defined what you are doing, you are prone to rationalizing it after the fact, even if you know it isn't perfect. This makes it harder to see better opportunities along the way. Before writing any code or hiring any programmers, start by validating that people desperately want what you plan to build and that you know how to get in front of these people.

Too many times I have seen people (including myself) waste months or years of their life building fields of dreams. When you build ideas before you test their viability, you are exposed to all the downside risk of wasting the full time and effort (and money) you put into it. When you test the viability of ideas before you build them, you preserve optionality and limit your downside risk to a small fraction of the effort it would take to fully build the idea.

In order to determine which ideas are worth testing in the first place, I have created a series of questions, designed to dig into my motivations for starting the company, determine whether the idea is in line with my core values, and help me determine whether I'm getting closer to finding something worth doing.

- Why do I want to start this company?
- Who's my target customer?
- What's their hair-on-fire problem?
- Is there an even bigger problem?
- What kind of startup do I want it to be?
- Does this company align with my core values?
- What do I specially bring to the table?
- Let's explore each of these questions in more detail.

1. WHY ARE YOU STARTING THIS COMPANY?

There's that pesky question again. Why do you want to start this business and how are you uniquely qualified to make it successful?

The first answer you might come up with is it seems like a fairly easy way to get rich. That's not a terrible motivation. Financial independence is a reason that many people want to start a business. Here's the problem though: there are many proven, more surefire ways to make money than doing a startup. Some examples include being a high-end and commercial real-estate agent, investment banker, lawyer, or doctor. Many of these professions involve far less risk than being a startup founder.

If your only motivation is money, you will likely be much happier if you pursue another way to get it. One of my best friends while growing up was only interested in getting money. After exploring law school and medical school, he ended up becoming a world-class professional poker player and has made more money than I have by a long shot.

So what else is there? What is it about startups and entrepreneurship that attracts you? What's drawing you to the idea of founding a company? What do you envision for yourself as an entrepreneur and why do you want it? And what makes you the right person to start this company? Why are you uniquely qualified to solve this problem?

These are hard questions to answer. And it's made harder once you realize you don't entirely know what's motivating you to start your own company, let alone *this particular company*. And that's okay. You don't need to know *why* right away. But asking yourself *why* is something you should be doing frequently.

Starting a business is a great opportunity for self-exploration; to get down deep inside and learn what makes yourself tick. It is an opportunity that a lot of startup founders miss because it's easy to feel too busy to stop and ask these questions. An entrepreneur I have great respect for once told me he learned through entrepreneurship that he had a burning and persistent need to see his ideas get into the hands of strangers and the general marketplace, and also to see the people around him share in that success. That's a great start, but where does the need come from? Why is it there?

The real and lasting rewards of entrepreneurship come from understanding yourself better as a human being. The pressure cooker environment that comes with founding a company will reveal a lot about yourself, and it can be one of the most valuable experiences of your life if you're open to it. As an added benefit, digging deep into your motivations will likely lead you to figure out your company's mission.

A mission is something deeper and far more meaningful than how to make money. A mission is about the specific value your customer receives when they come to you. A mission is why you do what you do.

Let's say you sell pesticides to farmers. If I ask you what your customers want, what would you say? Many people would answer: "My customers want to kill weeds." That's not it though. The value your customers get isn't killing weeds. They don't wake up every morning hoping to kill more weeds that day. They are hoping they will grow more crops. If your mission is to kill all the world's weeds, your mission is not aligned with your customer's mission. If you want to help the world grow more crops, you have now tapped into something bigger and more meaningful. You have aligned yourself with your customers' mission.

None of my early startup ideas had missions that were aligned with my customers. They were just ideas to make me money. For example, I once thought that I would create an online invoicing website for small businesses. Why? Because I saw FreshBooks online invoicing (which had just launched) seemed to be making money and getting press and attention. I thought I could build that pretty easily. I wasn't uniquely qualified to build an online invoicing app, I just thought it would be easy to copy.

A mission is the centerpiece of everything you're doing and will ultimately be what drives every decision you make for your startup. A mission will determine the product decisions, the marketing decisions, and the sales decisions; it will also be the driving force in the relationships you build with customers, investors, and your employees. And asking *why* is the first step toward finding it.

It is much easier to come up with a bad mission statement than a good one. Many entrepreneurs simply think about it for five minutes—eschewing the uncomfortable self-evaluation entirely—and write down:

"My mission is to change the world for the better."

Or:

"My mission is to improve people's lives."

That's not a mission. It's too generic and meaningless. Whose lives are you improving? Are you helping poor children in Africa? Wealthy Americans? In what way are you making the world better? It needs to be more specific.

"Okay then, my mission is to delight people by creating great software."

Nope, still not a mission. A mission needs missionaries. Is your mission something that your customers could believe in? What about strangers?

Imagine yourself walking up to somebody on the street, a perfect stranger, and asking, "Do you believe in [insert mission here]?" Under this simple question, the above examples fall apart immediately:

"So, do you believe in delighting people with great software?"

"Sorry dude, I don't have any spare change."

"Do you believe in changing the world?"

"Well, maybe, but what does that mean?"

Delighting people and changing the world is not something to *believe in*—it's too vague and broad, so it doesn't connect with people.

Now let's look at a couple examples from two of the top brands in the world and apply our test to them. Nike makes shoes but their mission is to promote an active lifestyle. So:

"Do you believe in promoting an active lifestyle?"

Some people might say "yes," others may say "no." But an active lifestyle is something you can believe in. That's a mission.

And if you believe in it, you can carry it with you into the world—you can become a missionary—and share that mission with others. The universality of Nike's message allows it to be adopted and personalized by its employees and its customers, who then go spread the word.

Apple's mission—*Think Different*—is similarly universal.

"Sure, I believe in thinking differently."

This mission empowers the thought leaders, the movers and shakers, the crazy ones. It empowers creative people and innovators. Apple's mission is about creating tools for visionaries—they just happen to make a phone. Creating a mission with this kind of specific universality sounds easy. It isn't. It's deceptively difficult, but it's incredibly important.

You might not figure out your company's mission on Day One, but if you commit to the journey, you will eventually get there. The process takes time. That's okay. There is plenty you can do to establish your company while you continue looking for your mission. Once it clicks, however, it will change everything. You will know it clicks because customers will start talking to their friends about your startup without you asking them to. Your waiting list will start growing out of control. People will become frothy and spend unimaginable time trying to get what you have made. Think of the people who stand in line for hours to get iPhones. When you figure out your mission and it clicks, that's the reward.

Once you find your mission, everything you have already created—all the product, content and assets you put together in the process of looking for your mission—can be repurposed. You can realize your *why* and clearly communicate it to others. If you truly believe in your mission, other people will respond.

Your best ideas, along with your great life missions, are deeply nestled within your background, your history, and your motivations for starting a company in the first place. But you have to look for them, like carefully digging up a fossil; and that means choosing to embrace the self-exploration process.

2. WHO'S YOUR TARGET CUSTOMER?

Who has the problem that you're trying to solve? Who exactly is your target customer? And don't tell me your business has something for everyone or that you have multiple customer profiles. Remember that Facebook started out limited to college students only. Tell me the one target customer you are after.

Specificity is key when determining your target customer. I have fallen for the temptation to try to serve multiple customers at the same time (developers AND enterprises, users AND advertisers, teens AND retirees, wedding couples AND wedding vendors) and it never worked. It is tempting because two-sided businesses seem two times as big. The problem is they are ten times as hard to build.

In the first few years of a startup, you can't be great at serving more than one kind of customer. You don't have the time, resources, money, or people to pull it off. You might be ok or maybe even good, but never great. Never truly exceptional. Which means your competition that focuses on just one side at a time will do a better job and build their business orders of magnitude faster than you.

Even at AppFog where I was able to sign up over a hundred thousand developers in a couple years, I could have done better. We split our focus and tried to simultaneously sell to developers and enterprises. Meanwhile, some of our competitors focused only on the developers who like low price points and never talk to sales people; they ended up signing up millions of those developers. Other competitors focused on enterprises with enormously long sales cycles, high-touch expectations, and cut-throat entrenched competition (a very different customer profile); these competitors sold more eight-figure deals than we could.

You have to pick a single target customer and focus on creating value for that one person. Nobody is immune to this rule. Nobody is clever enough to get around it on a technicality. Most two-sided businesses focus on one side first and build the other side after they have reached critical mass on the first side.

Once you have figured out who your customer is, it's time to learn everything you can about them. Understand their psychology as deeply as you would if you were an FBI profiler. *What are their hopes and dreams? What are their fears and frustrations? What do they read? Who influences them? What media do they consume? Where do they hang out? With whom?*

Once you've built your profile, you have to figure out how they will discover you. Are they going to read about you or find out about you from another business? Where do they go to find solutions to their problems? What websites do they visit every day? What kind of web searches do they perform? These are the places you will need to be showing up.

By attaining a deep understanding of your target customer, you will figure out what you need to do to connect with them. You will know how to be found, you will know how to speak to them, and you will understand their problems. Most importantly, you will know how to address their problems.

3. WHAT'S YOUR CUSTOMER'S HAIR-ON-FIRE PROBLEM?

Avoiding this question is the single biggest mistake I made time and again: *What's your target customer's most urgent, hair-on-fire problem?*

When analyzing your target customer's biggest problems, it is important to keep in mind that the real issue is not the problem that *you* think they have, it's the problem that *they* think they have. This is where I kept failing at making a successful business for years.

What do I mean by this? Let me tell you a story.

When my wife and I were about to get married, I had an idea for a new kind of wedding registry website. *I've already been living with my soon-to-be wife for years*, I thought. *We have pots, pans, and towels. We even have a gravy boat. We don't need traditional wedding registry stuff, we need help paying for the wedding.* My wife and I both agreed it would be amazing if we could register for our wedding photographer or parts of our honeymoon.

My thought process was: *Who is my target customer? Well, wedding vendors are the ones missing out on this revenue stream. They could be a making a ton of money off of a service like this!*

But instead of determining whether a missed revenue stream was the real hair-on-fire problem for my target customer, I moved straight into *How am I going to get people to sign up for this?* My solution was, *I'm going to have the wedding vendors set up their sites through my system, and then they will get their customers to set up registries.* The way I figured it, photographers, bakers, and travel agents see couples all the time. I would get these vendors to create their own registry site through which couples could sign up to register for the services they wanted. It would be a great channel. I believed I had figured it all out.

It should come as no surprise to you that the idea flopped.

Our gut instinct as entrepreneurs is to gravitate toward ideas that are so new, so groundbreaking and awesome that they don't solve problems that actually exist for the customer, at least not yet. This happens because we fundamentally believe that if we create something radically different it will add so much value that people will fall over backwards to give us money. They'll be so grateful that we've actually resolved a problem they didn't know they had that they will flock to us with cash in hand.

I thought the wedding vendors would be so excited I discovered a new way for them to make money that they would be lining up for my service.

Unfortunately, as entrepreneurs we're usually the only ones who can see the bigger picture and connect all the dots. I believed that the value proposition is bigger for problems that people didn't know they had. And maybe it was true, but usually the vast majority of those kinds of solutions are terrible ideas for startups.

Here's why: if people don't know that they need your solution, they will never think to look for it. If they aren't looking (actively or passively) for solutions to the problem you solve, you're never going to grow exponentially.

Now, I've had a guy come to me and say: "Lucas, but what about Twitter? Nobody was searching for ways to send 140-character messages to each other before Twitter existed." The problem that Twitter solves isn't how to send 140-character messages. The problem Twitter solved was one of communication. Twitter was just a better way to communicate with famous people. The problem of better communication has existed for as long as humanity has been writing on cave walls, and when people saw they could essentially text message with celebrities who would actually respond to them, it solved the hair-on-fire problem of fan mail in the digital age.

Unlocking the psychology behind your customer is key.

The same person tried to get me on this point again. He said, "Ok, you got me on Twitter, but what about Poo-Pourri, the viral success of an oil-based toilet water spray that eliminates bathroom odors by creating a water barrier? Who was looking for that problem? Nothing exactly like that existed before." Sure, there hadn't been a product you spray into the toilet bowl, but there have long been products to try to cover unpleasant bathroom odors in other ways. And when you hear about this idea where you use the natural property of oils by creating a vapor barrier on top of the water, it makes sense. Great products solve everyday problems ten times better than the things that have come before.

When I picked wedding vendors as my target customer, I got it all wrong. If I had taken the time to determine whether I was solving my target customer's hair-on-fire problem, I would have quickly realized that they didn't even know they were missing out on income through wedding registries. I had solved a problem they didn't know they had. And my solution wasn't clearly ten times better than any other way that vendors could try to make more money.

A year later, I saw a startup build on the same idea and it went gangbusters. It was a huge success. What did they understand that I didn't? The startup targeted the *wedding couples*, the people like me originally who actually had their hair on fire. This was a product ten times better than manually creating your own custom wedding registry.

I had come so close and, and if I had asked myself a few more fundamental questions, maybe I could have seen breakout success then too. How close might you be right now to finding your great idea? Unfortunately, it wasn't my time yet and I was still years away from finding my breakout success.

Here's a rule of thumb for you: if you can't determine the specific hair-on-fire problem your target customer has—their deep desire—chances are you're trying to serve the wrong type of customer.

4. IS THERE AN EVEN BIGGER PROBLEM?

Once you've identified your target customer and have successfully identified their hair-on-fire problem (the one they know they have), there is still one more question to ask: does your customer have a bigger problem you could solve?

This is an opportunity to really improve your understanding of the target customer. You have to understand not just the problem that you're trying to solve for them, but also the nine other problems on their Top Ten list.

If you don't know what those are, you should talk to your target customer and listen to their stories—you need to start building relationships. If your customer has a list of ten problems, they might only be looking for solutions to the first three. So if you focus on problem #4 you are likely to fail, regardless of how well you solve it.

You might find yourself thinking: *I can't solve that problem, my company isn't big enough and hasn't raised enough money.* That's a sign that you're probably on the right track. When you're turned off by an idea because it seems too big, too scary, or too hard, that's when you need to capitalize.

Is it a risk? Sure. While most people don't want to assume more risk than they have to, is that a valid reason to pursue a lesser idea? Not if it means the difference between solving your target customer's #1 problem instead of their #4 problem. Startups are about converting outsized risks into outsized returns. Most small businesses, on the other hand, are about reproducing well-known, well-understood business models for modest returns. If you have a million dollars in 2015, you can franchise a McDonald's store and make around a hundred to two hundred thousand dollars a year in profit. Not as much as you thought? A single McDonald's store doesn't have the potential to go public.

If you find yourself fizzling out over and over again when trying to come up with your next great startup idea, it might be because you are not thinking big enough. If you can't find a mission that a lot of people care about, it might be because the problems you are solving are too small. If you have trouble committing to an idea for more than a couple weeks or months, it might be because it doesn't even capture your own imagination at a deep enough level. The profit motive alone will try to trick you into thinking small. Short-term gains for a quick buck don't have staying power.

5. WHAT KIND OF STARTUP DO YOU WANT IT TO BE?

Another question I used to routinely avoid asking myself was what kind of startup I wanted to be down the road. Did I want to be bootstrapped or venture funded? Did I want to get a quick exit or go for an IPO? I used to go with whatever the wind blew, staying bootstrapped as it suited me or trying to raise some investment on a whim.

Long-term perspective becomes really key when you think about what kind of company you want to build. Do you want a lifestyle business or are you aiming to be a publicly traded billion-dollar business?

If your goal is just to start a business, there are many kinds of businesses out there. You could start a mom and pop shop. You could do a franchise business like a McDonald's. Each option has a different tradeoff. You need to determine what you want your company to be over the long term in order to put your attention in the right places from the very beginning.

For example, if you don't think you could ever take your company public, then not only do you not need for you to raise venture capital, you wouldn't succeed in raising money if you tried. Venture capitalists don't expect all their startups to go public, but they almost never invest in ideas that don't have the ability to one day.

Each kind of business entails a different growth process, so you want to make sure that the steps you are taking are in alignment with your goals. If you do want to raise venture capital, you should make sure your idea is big enough that it is worth investing tens of millions of dollars into. If you want to build a lifestyle business, then starting with a small idea isn't bad.

If you do want venture funding, it's very important that you understand the rules of that industry. Not only for your sake but also for the sake of everyone you're going to interact with. Venture capitalists are going to assess whether you fit the mold of someone who is successfully raising venture capital. If you don't, they're not going to invest in you, and they usually won't give you much feedback. They often hope that you figure it out on your own and come back to them when you do.

Entrepreneurs don't think about their startups from the

venture capitalist's point of view very often, but venture capitalists are in this for the long haul too. Often the perceived risk of burning a bridge, and thus future business potential, outweighs the value of constructive feedback.

Being a venture capitalist is not an easy job. VCs have to say no 999 times out of a thousand. Often, they can only make one or two investments a year. And they get pitched four or five times a day. They can't invest in every good idea they see. There is a long list of venture capital firms that didn't invest in Apple, Intel, Amazon, and every other big company you have heard of today. It's not a personal thing when they say no to you. You have to fit a pattern they're expecting to see and you have to have the motivation to keep going through rejection. If you don't know what motivations venture capitalists are looking for yet, you should learn them.

Set yourself up for success by determining what you want out of your business over the long term. Study the path of other people that have already gotten to where you want to be. Start following that path. It's okay if you don't think you know how yet. Start studying. It's as much about your personal growth and journey as it is about starting a company.

6. DOES THIS COMPANY ALIGN WITH YOUR CORE VALUES?

Core values are the foundation of your company. If you don't have a solid foundation, your organization will be much more prone to collapse. The way you're going to make it from a one-man operation to a company of twelve, forty, one hundred, or one thousand-plus employees is by determining the things you value the most and then adhering to them as things grow.

Core values are the things you deem most important in every facet of your life, the things you truly believe are essential to a well-lived life and a well-run company. Your core values are immutable, which makes them the perfect solid foundation for your startup because everything else is likely to change at some point. A solid base is fundamental to the health and stability of your company, especially when your environment is so dynamic and volatile.

As an example of how I could have used core values to my advantage was when I finally fired my first employee. I struggled to find the right words. My lawyers told me to keep my speech as short as possible and offer no explanation. This made sense to me intellectually, but emotionally it felt wrong. I hated myself. My heart was on the floor and my stomach was in my throat. I couldn't believe the things I said. What was I doing? How did things get so bad? Why was I even starting this company in the first place? I could have made the situation a lot easier for my employee and myself if I had created a culture based on core values. You have to do this early and re-enforce it often.

One of the earliest moments in my life where my core values were put to the test was during high school. Not many people know this now, but I was a major choir geek for most of my childhood. The kind that went to international choir competitions. We had a wonderful director too, Laurie Gutormson. She was as much a natural charismatic hard-nosed leader as she was a music teacher. Some people look up to their football coaches as their mentors. For others, it might be their track or wrestling coaches. For me, my high school coach was my choir director.

In my senior year of high school, Laurie was diagnosed

with breast cancer. Our small men's choir was supposed to fly to Vienna to compete in a prestigious international competition that year. However Laurie's health deteriorated to the point that it was clear she couldn't travel. Some of Laurie's most prized core values were courage, determination, and hard work. She beat it into every one of us at least twice a week. She wasn't going to let her illness get in the way of our success.

We ended up going to Austria without our beloved director. The trip started strong with a little sightseeing before the competition, but when you put a group of seventeen-year-old guys in a foreign country with little adult supervision, things go sour quickly. A couple boys were caught drinking in a bar after curfew and all mayhem broke loose. Emotions ran high and for a while, it seemed we all forgot why we were there in the first place.

Then we got a call. Laurie had taken a turn for the worse and they didn't know if she would still be alive by the time we got home. I still remember talking to her that night and wishing her well. A few of us sung her favorite song to her, the Ave Maria by Franz Biebl. She couldn't say much, but I could hear her soft smile.

The next day, as we began our rehearsals, we lost our way. But we rallied strong and practiced maniacally until we knew every last chord by heart. It was because we were guided by the core values Laurie had lovingly instilled in us: courage, determination, and hard work.

Although we performed without our director (at least physically), we won the first prize. We brought the trophy home to Laurie who had lived just long enough for us to share it with her. She passed away a few short weeks later, but her core values live on in all of us to this day.

Everybody has a unique set of core values. Maybe you have already identified what yours are and how they might fit into the foundation of your company. If you haven't, I encourage you to do so. Once you have determined the values that are most important in your life, weigh them against your startup idea. Is your idea in alignment with your core values? If your idea violates any of your values—even if it's a gray area—it is not the right idea for you.

If you don't know your core values off the top of your head, choose four to eight from the list (or any others you can come up with) and create a personal acronym. You will refer back to this later many times.

Adventure	Freedom	Knowledge
Balance	Frugality	Peace
Confidence	Fulfillment	Power
Control	Fun	Progress
Courage	Growth	Reason
Creativity	Hard work	Resourcefulness
Determination	Happiness	Security
Discipline	Health	Self-reliance
Education	Hope	Service
Ethics	Honesty	Strength
Faith	Humor	Success
Family	Independence	Truth
Financial security	Integrity	Wisdom
Friendship	Kindness	

I know this might sound corny right now. I know that when I first heard the idea I rolled my eyes. But it works.

These ideas are grounded in well-tested principles that will help you down the road in countless ways. No matter how big your urge is to skip this part because you think you don't need it, resist that temptation.

As an example, if you happen to strongly believe in the core values of Creativity, Happiness, Adventure, Service, and Ethics, your acronym might be CHASE. You can make sure everyone who works at the company shares these values and honors and enforces them. If you make it clear up front that repeated violation of core values will lead to termination, then firing people can become much less personal (me firing you) and more issues based (culture doesn't fit).

Begin by determining your core values for yourself, writing them down, and committing to adhering to them in all of the decisions you make. This will ensure that the organization you build is one you can be proud of. Set these up front and never change them. Repeat them often and you will be much better prepared for many difficult moments in building a great business.

7. WHAT DO YOU SPECIALLY BRING TO THE TABLE?

When weighing your startup ideas, it is also essential to determine if your idea is in line with your own personal strengths. To put it simply: *why are you uniquely the right person to start this company?*

If I had asked myself why I was the right person to start an online invoicing system years ago, I might have realized how opportunistic I was being and saved myself a lot of time. My online invoicing idea was doomed to failure because I had no real strengths or points of view to bring to an invoicing business. I was just doing it because I thought it would be an easy way to make money. I thought it would be easy passive income.

It was only when I focused on a startup idea where my specific background (being a professional PHP programmer for eight years) gave me unique insight, perspective, and knowledge that not every entrepreneur out there had, that I created a startup that could really succeed.

Of course you won't be strong in every area of your developing startup, you're going to have to learn a lot. I learned about hosting Java and doing enterprise software sales, which I had been totally ignorant of before. But you will be in a much stronger position if your natural and professional strengths are in line with the company you want to build.

Write down your strengths and weaknesses. All of them. And when you can't think of any more, hand the list to your spouse or close friends and give them carte blanche to assess you with brutal honesty. Try to put fifty items in each column.

Once you have your list, begin to look for the strengths that are most aligned with your startup idea—how can you leverage these strengths to best benefit your startup? If you are making leaps and generalizations to force it, maybe this startup idea just isn't suited to you after all.

Then evaluate the weaknesses and ask yourself what kind of people do you need to make this idea a reality? Many founders by default want to be the CEO simply for the prestige of the title. If you realize that people skills like sales and talking to investors are just not your thing, realize that you might be better suited as the CTO or maybe the CMO and there is nothing wrong with that.

Everybody has weaknesses. Most people don't have to confront their weaknesses often because they avoid them. You can't afford to avoid your weaknesses because you will be wearing too many hats. So it is better to examine your weaknesses closely and create strategies to compensate for them.

By measuring your weaknesses against the needs of your startup, you will be able to figure out where your biggest hiring needs are. Build a team that is strong where you are weak, and learn from them to make yourself stronger and more well rounded.

After asking yourself all these questions, you now have a solid foundation for a great startup:

- A big problem
- A clear solution
- A story for how your customer will find out about your company
- Why you are ideally suited to start this company
- What kind of company you are building and its core principles
- Key weaknesses identified, which you will need to build a great team around you

Without knowing it, by this point if you have answers to all these questions, you have created the start of a terrific investor pitch before you have even officially started your company. These are the same things every investor looks for in a great pitch.

This is not an accident. Far too many founders fall in love with their ideas early and only after it is too late do they try to retrofit venture capital on ideas that are not investable.

I made this mistake many times myself. It is always better to start with an idea that has the potential to be investible than to try to blindly convince someone that your idea deserves investment.

Seven Things I Wish Someone Had Told Me Earlier

There are some key things about starting a business that are fundamentally true, things that took me a long time to realize on my own. Things that I wish someone had told me earlier. And it's possible that someone did. The fact is, sometimes the things that you need to hear most are the hardest to understand. Throughout my career, I received—and promptly ignored—a lot of great advice. I later wished that I hadn't. Some of these things I wasn't ready to hear, and some I would only come to learn were true later on.

Of course there is so much to learn over the course of founding a company—on both a business level and a personal one. It's enough information to fill hundreds of books. Still, these seven lessons were the ones that have proven themselves true time and time again throughout my career.

1. YOUR STARTUP IS A REFLECTION OF YOU

One of the most impactful things I learned is that your startup is a reflection of you. This can either scare or empower you.

Your startup is a reflection of everything in your life that has brought you to this point. Everything that you've done in your life has led you to create this company. The person you are led you to choose which idea to pursue; your goals, your experience, and your work ethic will all show through in the company you build. The ups and downs of your startup will highlight what you are doing right, but they will also lay bare your flaws.

If you're only starting a company to get rich and if your thinking is measured purely in short-term gains, then your startup is going to reflect that and lack authenticity. If you are chasing a market opportunity that doesn't solve a real problem, then your startup is going to reflect the fact that you haven't fully developed your concept.

For example, let's say that you're a programmer like me. You've been programming for a long time and want to use those skills to develop a startup. So you run through some ideas and decide to build an invoicing company. Why? Well mostly because invoicing is easy, people need it, and you think you'll make lots of money doing it. At least that's what I thought when I did it.

That kind of thinking will cause problems immediately. I had no passion for invoicing. I wasn't trying to solve a problem that exists in the invoicing market. Rather, I was simply trying to profit off of an industry that I perceived to be easy money. A startup like this has no soul and all potential customers will see that. If your mission is to snare customers and take their money by any means necessary, you are set up for failure.

Conversely, if you are working to solve a very real prob-lem—something you are authentically passionate about—that will be just as palpable to your target customer, employees, and investors. Authenticity about who you are, what you're trying to do, and why you're doing it is what will build the relationship between you and those you are trying to connect with. When you bring together everything you have learned, everything you have failed at, everything you have succeeded at, all of your passions, and it becomes clear that *this* is what you should be doing, it is incredibly powerful and compelling. It will empower you and it will attract others.

It is important to note that, while your startup is a reflec-tion of you, it does not define you. It can be very difficult to separate the success or failure of your company from who you are as a person, but it is crucial that you learn to do so. Failure isn't personal, it's expected from even the best entrepreneurs. It's guaranteed that you will experience setbacks. It's up to you whether you see them as growth opportunities rather than losses. Nobody thinks a wounded soldier is a failed soldier, but rather a hero. Treat your startup wounds like a soldier would: a point of pride. For the same reason, it's really poor form and bad karma to pick on fellow entrepreneurs (even your competitors) when they hit misfortune in any form.

If you're in the middle of failure or if you have failed at building a company already, try to reframe the experience in a positive light by learning from it. When you look back and figure out what went wrong, apply those lessons to your future endeavors. That is a reflection of you persevering, and it means that your next startup is going to be stronger. After all, expecting to find success without failure is like expecting to look like a bodybuilder after one day at the gym. It just doesn't work that way. You have to be ready for the long-term commitment and the long-term thinking that goes into it.

Bodybuilders aren't terrible at lifting weights if they get injured now and again. Injuries happen while lifting heavy things. Yet, if something goes wrong with your startup there is a common inclination to say to yourself, "I'm a terrible entrepreneur." Your startup is a reflection of you, but its failure does not mean that you are a failure. It takes a lot of repetition and often some setbacks to get where you want to be. That's okay. Failures and injuries happen. Rest, recover, and come back stronger.

Should you experience setbacks, a level of honesty is required to analyze the reasons. Did you approach your startup with the proper long-term mentality? Were you just chasing a quick buck? You need to be honest about what your intentions were for your company and learn from any flaws you find therein.

Look hard at yourself in the mirror, both physically and mentally. You are the heart of your company, and a good look at yourself will reveal the pulse of everything going on around you. The converse is true too. Take good care of yourself if you want to give your company its best chance at success. Your startup is a reflection of you and you are a reflection of your startup. Whether it succeeds or fails, make sure it is something you can be proud of.

2. NEVER VIOLATE YOUR CORE VALUES

If your startup is a reflection of you, it's also a reflection of your core values. Just as you should never violate your core values, your startup should abide by the same rule. Unless your core values are selfishness and rude behavior, you should always stick to them. Especially when you find yourself in the following scenarios:

- Determining who will work for your company. You must hire and fire employees based on your core values.
- Determining whether to pursue certain deals. You must turn down short-term opportunities (customers, revenue, or business deals) that violate your core values.
- Determining where your money comes from. You must not take investment from any source that goes against your core values.

As you build your startups, you will often be tempted to stray from your core values. Sometimes it may feel as if the fate of the world depends on you violating your core values. Decisions may be especially difficult when you feel you are walking away from what you think you want most. Just remember: there is no such thing as a must-do deal.

Investments are more than putting a check in the bank, and it's more than someone believing in your company enough to help fund it. Money initiates relationships. Accepting an investment is also accepting a relationship with the investor. Once you cash the check, the person who wrote it becomes a part of your team, and you become accountable to that person. It's more than a fiduciary commitment—it's a partnership. This is why it's so important to never violate your core values to secure investment. If the potential investor is someone you cannot see yourself working with for years, then you shouldn't take their money. If their values do not align with yours, or if you don't think they will support your value-based decisions in difficult times, then you shouldn't take their money.

The same can be said about your customers. It's never easy to turn down business, but listen to your gut instincts. If a customer is wrong for you, your gut will tell you to walk away regardless of the size of the check. You can choose to deny those feelings and move forward anyway (the short-term solution), or you can ask yourself why you're struggling with the decision in order to determine what is bothering you. By giving yourself time to reflect, you might realize that you're about to violate a core value by entering into business with the wrong kind of customer.

Of course, it's not always that simple. You may be faced with a choice between taking on a customer that would violate your core values and having to close or downsize. In this kind of situation, it's very easy to rationalize: "If I only go against my values this one time, maybe I can keep the lights on..." Short-term thinking and "easy money" always contain hidden debts that are hard to repay. Once you violate your core values and initiate a relationship with a customer, every future action within that relationship represents a broken promise to yourself—a Faustian pact.

No one contract is a must-sign contract. Do not take money in any form from the wrong people.

Core values can also bring hard decisions to a head when dealing with employees. It is critical that the core values of your company be explained to each employee on day one. Unfortunately, in a dynamic environment that doesn't always happen. There's no better day than today to fix that.

Why is it so important to reinforce core values early and

often? Sometimes you'll be so focused on running and building your business that you'll suddenly realize that one of your top employees is a bad fit. He might be your star programmer, but he's dragging down the rest of your team by being negative or demoralizing. It's a hard lesson to learn, and I wish someone had told me this earlier, but not firing someone who should be fired is the type of thing that can ruin an organization. Your best employees will not stick around very long waiting for you to take action, and if a startup is only as good as its people, then keeping rotten apples too long is a way to ruin the whole batch.

It is much easier to deal with problems that may arise with employees if the company's value system is explained clearly from the get-go. Then, you can remind difficult employees about your conversations in regards to the core values of your company. You can point to some examples of their actions that stand in violation of those core values and remind them that without corrective action, they will need to leave.

Using core values as the center of your criticisms can be useful in delivering this message without personally attacking those difficult employees. You can say: "This kind of behavior might be totally fine at most companies, but we are trying to cultivate something different here." Notice that you are acknowledging that the behavior (and by extension the employee as a person) isn't necessarily bad. Instead, you are making a point that it's just not a fit for your company.

Now, you might be thinking, *Well, great, but my company culture is already established. I'm not a hundred percent happy with it, but what can I do now? Seems like I am too late.* It's never too late to re-establish culture and set core values. If things have already spun out of control, it's time to have a serious meeting with your employees. This meeting is more important than product deadlines, customers, revenue growth, or anything else. You may want to go somewhere offsite to magnify its importance. Here is a script you can use:

"I called this meeting because I messed up recently and I need to fix it. It is incredibly important we reset expectations about acceptable behavior, because I have not done a good job communicating our company's core values. I want to share with you some things I believe in and things this company was founded upon: honesty, integrity, and hard work. I think some of them have been violated recently, and that stops now. I won't point names or place blame. I have as much blame as anyone else here because I have let it get this far. But that stops today. These values need to be at the center of all further action, and if anyone finds this to be unacceptable, it's time for you to leave this team. Can each and every one of you either commit to these core values while at work or hand in their resignation to me by the end of the week?"

Be frank and upfront about your expectations, and most importantly, hold your employees accountable from that moment forward. You don't need to flog poor behavior publicly, but you can't let people off the hook any longer. You will need to call people into your office and have one-on-one difficult conversations until people realize how serious you are about this.

As a leader, you are responsible for communicating core values to your employees on a regular basis. By clearly laying them out, you're reinforcing what you stand for, what you want your company to be, and what you expect from those who work for you. This message becomes fortified by your choices of leaders. It comes through in how you manage your team and with whom you do business. By only accepting business and investment that match your values, you will allow your startup to stay true to your mission and to grow in the direction of your long-term thinking.

Your core values are the *keystone* of your leadership success. They have to be strong in order for your organization to be strong, and they must be defended even if the cost is great. After all, the expense of violating them is far worse.

Begin by determining your core values for yourself, writing them down, and committing to adhering to them in all the decisions you make. This will ensure that you can be proud of the organization you lead and the team you manage. Once you establish your core values, live them, revisit them, and *never* stray from them. Remind yourself of them often and you will be much better prepared for the many difficult moments inevitable in growing a great organization.

3. YOU ARE NOT YOUR THOUGHTS

Your thoughts are amazingly powerful. After all, they came up with your startup in the first place. But often people confuse their thoughts with themselves. When you say, "I am afraid, I shouldn't do this or that," you are identifying yourself with your thoughts.

Most people never realize that their own thoughts are often little more than an endless string of blabbering garbage that is often short sighted and wrong. Your thoughts (not funding or customers or product problems) are often the single biggest obstacle in your path to starting your business.

If I had listened to my thoughts about starting AppFog, I would have never quit my day job. After all, I was working at a steady job earning the highest salary I had ever made. I was the sole breadwinner for my family. My wife was pregnant with our first child and due to deliver in three months.

My thoughts were constantly revolting. Every morning, the same messages rang through my head: *This is stupid. I should quit. I'm a failure. This is going to end terribly, just as every other idea I have ever had did.* Every self-defeating thought you can imagine echoed between my ears. As my savings dwindled and I moved closer and closer to bankruptcy, my thoughts became louder and more persuasive. It felt crippling as I began to doubt every decision I made as I was making it.

Even with such terrible thoughts, I kept aggressively moving forward with AppFog. I had four thousand people signed up, and things had progressed so well that the time had come for me to choose between the security of a steady salary and the high upside of the startup.

Clearly I chose the startup, but even after making that choice, the voices wouldn't stop complaining. *Go back to a regular day job. You should really get health insurance before your son arrives in the world. You can't really do this.* The incessant brain chatter didn't stop even after raising millions in venture capital.

I used to believe that the things going around in my head were me, that my thoughts defined me as a person. It's easy to feel this way; most of the time your thoughts have valid sounding points. They are clever and have a knack for saying things that are true (at least locally true, though they often miss the bigger picture), which understandably makes you inclined to believe them. I was afraid that I had made a mistake; even worse, I was afraid that I had permanently hurt my family by making the wrong choice.

It was while panicking that I was finally able to realize my mistake: I was allowing my thoughts to control me. My mistake wasn't in having the thoughts, but by letting them have the steering wheel. This realization came when I found myself observing my own thoughts from afar. Ironically, the thoughts were so potent, loud, and negative that I was jarred into noticing they were more of a reflex than anything else.

You are not your thoughts. You can treat your thoughts as a body part like a heart or a lung. You can't get rid of them and they obviously provide positive value to your life. But you must never abdicate your choices to your thoughts alone. Fighting negative thoughts only puts more undue focus on them and gives them more power. Scolding yourself for thinking you can't do something only feeds the negative thought cycles. It doesn't conquer them.

Another way to view it is like sitting in a movie theater. Your thoughts are like an endless stream of movies being projected onto a screen. Sometimes there are dramatic thoughts, other times there are scary thoughts, and yet other times there might be romantic thoughts. If the heroine is about to fall into a trap and you start yelling at the screen to tell her to stop, not only does it not help the heroine, but you have completely forgotten that you are just sitting in a theatre and can get up and walk out at any time. You have abdicated your choices by becoming engrossed in your head.

To conquer negative thoughts, you must first embrace them. You have to acknowledge them, give them a hug, and give them respect and peaceful attention. If your thoughts are screaming about how your startup is not going to work, start by acknowledging the fear. Then stand up, walk out of the theater letting the film continue, and make your choice independent of the incessant yapping. *I hear these thoughts and yet I'm going to continue because I believe in this idea.*

Thoughts obsess exclusively around past and future events—'what if' scenarios and regrets: *I regret hiring that programmer. I regret taking an investment from that venture capital firm. I regret launching the product too early. I regret waiting so long to launch.* These things already happened and can't be changed. *What if I can't get introduced to any VCs or what if I get introduced and they don't like me? What if my head programmer quits? What if my main customer quits? What if I can't make payroll. What will people think of me if I fail? What if people don't give me money?* These things haven't happened yet and may never happen.

Who cares what other people will think? What's the real downside? Trying to control what other people think of you is a fragile loser's game. The only healthy way to live is to stay true to yourself, to be a lighthouse, and to let others come and go as they please. You will naturally attract those who like the light and repel those who prefer the darkness. Sometimes this means you might repel those who are even close to you, maybe some family members. This is natural. You can never please everyone, but some people spend their lives trying to instead of realizing their own potential. Go forth and prove people wrong.

There is nothing intrinsically wrong with 'what if' scenarios and regrets. In fact, they can be very healthy in small doses. Protecting your downside is a critical task for any startup founder. The killer problem is that thoughts have a tendency to feed on each other exponentially. This leads you to spending massively outsized amounts of time obsessing about things that might not happen and things that can't be changed.

If you let you let your thoughts stay in the driver's seat of your actions, it's like the annoying high-pitched echoing squeal you get when you put a speaker next to a microphone.

One antidote to a negative-thinking feedback loop is focusing on the present moment. The one thing thoughts are most allergic to is living life fully right now. What in this moment is wrong? Use this question as a guide post. There are hundreds of potential disasters hiding around every corner: insolvency, mutiny, sabotage, etc. But what in this moment is wrong? Are you starving to death? Are you being tortured by a psychopath? Is a family member dying? Do you not have a roof over your head? Do you have no friends and loved ones (even if you don't always treat them that way)?

Another antidote to negative thinking is gratitude. Actively cultivating gratitude by looking for the things that are good in your life can bring you back to the present moment and provide much-needed perspective. Gratitude is like a pesticide to the weeds of negative thoughts. Maybe there is someone in your life who is really good at giving you perspective. How do they do that? Usually by showing you things to be grateful for. Practice that skill and you can be the one in your life who gives you perspective.

An advanced and even more highly potent form of gratitude is to have gratitude for the things going wrong in your life right now. Gratitude for having enough food to eat is easy. Gratitude for not being able to secure venture capital can be hard. But if you can practice that kind of gratitude, you gain a deeper perspective about the interconnectedness of complex systems. During the late '90s, the startup founders who sold their companies early for modest sums were laughed at by founders raising seemingly endless amounts of money. Then the bubble burst and left the laughing founders bankrupt. How quickly the tides can turn in life, and turn bad things good and good things bad. Only unlimited time and perspective can judge whether an action was right or wrong, good or bad.

There are physical antidotes to negative thinking as well. Yoga, acupuncture, massage, hot/cold baths, and meditation are excellent techniques for quieting your mind. But maybe those aren't your cup of tea? Try weight lifting, running, high-intensity interval training, sports, or Pilates (which is just a more cardio-active form of yoga). Physical activity is a fantastic way to reset your thought circuits. All of these activities create a distance between your "thoughts speaker" and your "thoughts microphone," and allow you to mentally reset.

When you put your "thoughts speaker" next to your "thoughts microphone," you can quickly forget all the things to have gratitude for in your life. The feedback loop drowns out and disproportionally and systematically makes mountains out of molehills. What happens if the company fails? What's the real downside risk? Will you die? Will you starve? Will your family starve? Probably not. You will probably either just get another job or start another company. That's not as dramatic as it seems in your head, but it's the truth.

The most personally transformative part of starting a company was realizing that the things I thought were not me, and that I didn't have to always listen to my own thoughts. In fact, if I had listened closely to my fears—if I identified and let my fears drive on autopilot—I would have never moved forward. You are not your thoughts. Make an effort to figure out what works to calm you down in high-stress situations.

Find a way to draw yourself into the present and away from your negative thoughts. Learn to objectively observe the terrifying soundtrack in your mind. Courage isn't the absence of fear. Courage is acknowledging your fear and moving forward anyway.

4. YOUR PRODUCT IS NOT YOUR COMPANY

Focusing holistically on your company instead of blindly on your product is a key mark of a craftsman founder. A product-obsessed founder will tinker with his or her product forever and never try to charge for it, perpetually afraid of what might happen if he or she asked someone for money for it.

Startup craft is about building businesses, not just products. A product is just a manifestation of a business, and not even a necessary one. Many businesses never sell products. Like a barbershop: you don't leave with something in your hands, yet they still generate value and compel your business. They sell services.

Building a business is about solving problems for people; products are only one way to accomplish that goal. This was a hard lesson for me to learn, especially coming from a software programming background. In the software industry, many people confuse the product with the company, and whatever that product is designed to do is the core value. This is flawed and shortsighted thinking; the product cannot be the only way that you're solving problems for the market.

DigitalOcean is a startup that has recently been called the third largest cloud service (behind Amazon and Google). Yet their product provides a tiny fraction of the feature-set of its rivals. Essentially all it does is give you virtual machines. Amazon has fifty-plus add-on services and Google is rapidly catching up. How do you explain this? If the DigitalOcean product was the company, they wouldn't stand a chance. But the DigitalOcean founders realize that the service they provide is about much more than their limited product. That's why they have invested in over fifty thousand detailed tutorials about how to do common system administration tasks. They even have a bounty and will pay you to write tutorials for them. Search for almost any Linux-related problem, and chances are very good you will find DigitalOcean as a first-page top result in Google. These tutorials are absolutely free, but at the bottom there is a clear call to action to try the tutorial on DigitalOcean. They are growing their business by solving the problems of system administrators on a broader scale through educational efforts rather than a feature war.

Your business is how you engage with your customer, which should go far beyond the product you are actually selling. Solving problems is your founder craft, building products is just one aspect of the craft. If you think your craft is limited to building products, you are acting like van Gogh (who didn't sell a single painting in his lifetime). However, if you think that solving someone's problems is your craft, you will approach things very differently. It is the value that you are delivering to your customers that is the most important part of building a business.

5. YOU DON'T HAVE TO FIGURE IT ALL OUT UP FRONT

I used to hold myself back with the thought that I didn't know all the answers up front. You don't have to wait until you have your best idea to get started. You don't have to wait until you've determined how you're going to build your crazy idea to start building strategic relationships. Founding a company is a journey, and if you sit and plan for too long you never really get started.

Although early decisions for your company can have a long-term impact, it doesn't mean you're locked into the choices you make forever. In fact, one of the worst mistakes a startup founder can make is falling in love with their own idea too early. This removes positive optionality for something ten times better than what you are doing right now. The key is to leave yourself flexibility; don't box in your startup so much that you can't change it if you need to. It's ok to move forward with an idea that you know will be different later. The trick is to not remove upside optionality.

One of my personal mentors, Dave Hersh, started a company called Jive Software. After only seven years, Jive IPOed and became a publicly traded billion dollar company. Yet over the course of its development, Jive underwent three complete changes of the entire business model. Dave and his team kept an open mind to optional ideas and completely re-invented themselves three times during those seven years. This meant letting go of revenue-paying customers because he no longer wanted to offer the services they still wanted.

If Dave had fallen in love with his first idea and held on to it—if he refused to examine new possibilities and different directions, or if he had adhered to early products that still had demand—he would have eliminated optionality. He wouldn't have created the service that eventually went public. Many founders fall in love with their idea so deeply they're not even open to other ideas. They're not looking for a better idea. Always look for better ideas throughout the whole process. There will always be great new directions and bigger opportunities.

I had an experience similar to Dave's when I shifted my company from a single programming language hosting service to a multiple programming language service. When I started, I didn't wait to figure out up front how to support Java and Python and Node (programming languages that I was not familiar with yet). I simply focused on one language I could do well: PHP.

Similarly, Instagram started out as an HTML5-based check-in app called Burbn. They didn't figure out up front how to make the best photo-sharing app in the world—that wasn't their goal. But when they noticed that photo sharing was the biggest part of Burbn, they didn't stay married to their first idea.

You don't have to have everything figured out before you start your company. You can use your uncertainty as an advantage by making choices that allow your startup all the flexibility it needs to be re-invented. Don't worry that you haven't figured out all the details yet. Start with doing one thing really well and adjust. Just keep moving forward and testing.

6. STARTUPS ARE ALL ABOUT RELATIONSHIPS, PEOPLE, AND STORIES

The best thing you can do to move your company forward is to build relationships. Startups are all about relationships, people, and stories. If you focus on those areas, you will be at a huge advantage over the long term.

Building relationships can seem daunting when you are just getting started. When I started, I didn't have any relationships with investors. Recently there has been a flood of incubators and accelerators promising to help you rapidly create your investor network. First-time founders are starting to believe that getting into an accelerator is somehow necessary to kick-start their entrepreneurship career. Nassim Taleb in *Antifragile* would call this teaching birds how to fly.

Taleb's fable starts with putting a group of professors in front of a flock of birds and lecturing the birds on the physics and aerodynamics of flying. At the end of the lecture, the professors open the cage and the birds fly, and the professors pat themselves on the back and publish papers on the effectiveness of their teachings.

How do you think entrepreneurs met investors before accelerators? Very few people wake up in the morning to find a fully formed personal network under the pillow—they have to build it. Fortunately, building relationships is very simple and not at all what most accelerators teach. Many accelerators shove dozens or even hundreds of new people in your face very quickly, which leads to shallow one-sided short-term experiences. I have been introduced to countless founders through accelerators. I hear from them once, they ask me for a favor, and then they disappear.

The big secret to building authentic relationships (with investors, advisors, customers, and anyone at all) is to give more than you get. Understand people—their hopes, dreams, and stories. Then help them get what they want. That is how you build authentic relationships with people. That's how it's been done for centuries. It's simple, but not easy. It takes a lot of work. Many accelerators keep you so busy with busywork that you simply don't have time to create authentic relationships with the people you meet.

Sometimes it's just a matter of reaching out and saying:

"Hey, I've been inspired by [INSERT THEIR PRODUCT/WRITING HERE]. I've used it to [INSERT ACTION HERE] and it worked really well."

Look for ways you can help them out. If they are an entrepreneur, maybe you can write a guest post for their blog. If they are an investor, try learning about them. Study companies they have invested in. Get to know the entrepreneurs they invested in who might be easier to connect with. If they have a blog or have been interviewed on a podcast, read it. Take a real interest.

A very effective technique for creating a relationship with someone is to ask:

"Hi again, I've enjoyed learning [INSERT LEARNING HERE] from you. But I'm running into difficulty because of [INSERT PROBLEM HERE]. Can you give me some pointers or maybe some books that could help?"

Then follow up and use the opportunity as a foot in the door.

Another technique for creating relationships is to become a customer for a service the person provides. Providing insightful ideas and promoting their company is a great way to give more than you get. Retweeting and contextually promoting their company on social networks is another way to get yourself on their radar. If they have recently written a book, you can offer to buy a bunch of copies and do a promotional giveaway to raise awareness of it. These kinds of things set you apart.

There is a huge difference between building an authentic relationship with someone and calling up an acquaintance, saying, "Hey, you're a startup guy, right? I'm wondering if you could introduce me to some investors." You have to honestly want to enter into a relationship with this other person. If you're just out to move your widget as fast as possible or score a cheap introduction to someone else, your intent will be transparent to other people.

Once you've empathized with someone, helped them, and created an honest relationship, they will naturally be more prone to helping you. That's reciprocity. Great entrepreneurs have a knack for it, but anyone can get better at it. If you help others, they may help you back in unexpected ways you might never expect.

7. GET READY FOR THE LONG HAUL

"Most people overestimate what they can do in one year and underestimate what they can do in ten years."

— BILL GATES

Take a moment right now to look back five or ten years ago at your life situation. How different are things now? Could you have imagined just five years ago that your life would be like this right now? If not, then how do you expect to be able to imagine what your life could be like five years from now?

There is a pervasive myth in the startup world that if you try to cram a lifetime of work into a year or two, all of a sudden you'll make thirty million dollars selling your company to

Google. Does that happen sometimes? Yes. Do some people win also thirty million dollar lotteries? Yes. That doesn't make a trend and is not a system you can rely on.

The average time to liquidity for a startup founder isn't eighteen months. It is seven to ten years. When you hear about early exits in the news, ignore them. They are useless noise. In fact, it's a good idea to ignore all news. The press systematically overemphasizes outliers and you can't count on being an outlier. Good investors know that it takes seven to ten years for great outcomes, and generally won't expect you to aim for or get an early exit. Some investors have even been known to block acquisitions that would make the founder rich because they want to hold out for more.

Furthermore, the average successful startup founder might create three to four long-term companies during his or her career; and two or three of them will probably fail. So, in reality, the average founder should be thinking about a thirty-year period, not just ten years. If this scares you, then startups might not be for you, after all.

There is no gold rush. There is no right or wrong time to start a company. There are no get-rich-quick schemes to follow that really work. You can't bet on early exits. Do some people get them? Yes. But some people win the lottery too.

A true craftsman doesn't cut corners in the name of short-term gains. If you're willing to take advantage of everyone you find in order to receive short-term benefit, people will remember that. Your actions follow you in unexpected ways. Both the good actions and the bad actions. Then down the road, when you are ready to sell your company, guess who might be sitting at the other side of the table? Murphy's law puts good money on the guy you screwed at the beginning of your career.

Don't leave a trail of bad karma in your path. Your behavior and the way you do business follows you. Always keep a long-term perspective. You're not counting the months to acquisition, you are building a career that could end up being more valuable than any one of the companies you start.

Seven Ways to Manage Founder Psychology

Being a founder is hard and painful. Over the long course of your career, you are very likely to get overwhelmed and burned out well before you see any life-changing money. Building a company out of an idea is the professional equivalent of throwing yourself into a crucible: high heat and high pressure over an extended period of time means you're either going to melt or emerge different on the other side.

You can set yourself up for success over the long term by learning to maintain and manage your mind.

This means thinking and acting like a successful leader even if you have only one employee and a small handful of cash from friends and family. When you're just getting your company off the ground, you will probably have to wear every hat and handle every issue, big or small, yourself. Your startup is going to feel like the only thing you should pay attention to, at the expense of yourself and personal relationships.

That's normal, but it doesn't make it right. You will face

a lot of rejection, especially in the early stages, but you can build resilience against failure. The efforts you make to frame your psychology for success in a leadership role will benefit you and your company over the long term.

As your startup begins to grow, so will the demands on your time and attention. As the responsibilities of managing a team of people and rolling out new products adds more bulk to your existing workload, it becomes more difficult to determine where your energy and time needs to be. By building and managing a strong founder's psychology in advance, you will be better prepared to put your focus on the right things, determine which problems you need to solve, and when and how to solve them.

What are the most important things for you to do as a leader as your company grows and changes? What should you prioritize most? What is your time actually worth? Here are a few of the things I have learned the hard way.

TECHNIQUE #1: TAKE CARE OF YOURSELF

Many of you reading this will roll your eyes and want to check Facebook instead of read about how to take better care of yourself. But hear me out, give me a chance to change your mind about the importance of self-care.

There is a mythical machismo belief in Silicon Valley that you must invest every waking hour and sacrifice every close relationship in order to find success in startups. I certainly followed this advice for many years. There was an extended point in my career where I was working from 7 a.m. to 2 a.m. every day of the week. If you believe these charlatan investors are encouraging this behavior, you might even think that I was doing this while running my company (since it was, after all, a successful exit).

The only thing I got from working that hard was fired. As common sense will tell you, there is only so long you can push yourself at full capacity before things start falling apart. If you don't believe me, feel free to try it yourself. Maybe you are trying it already.

Founding your company is going to be one of the most stressful things that happens in your career and, potentially, your entire life. Living with too much stress for too long will corrode your general health and wellbeing to the point that the tradeoff might not be worth it if you are not careful. Therefore, prioritizing your health is of critical importance. If you don't take care of yourself, then you're putting your entire company at risk.

Your startup is a reflection of you. So if you're working yourself to death, you're working your company to death. Especially in the beginning when it's very likely that your company is just you. If you're not healthy, your company is not healthy. You must actively prioritize caring for yourself in the following three ways:

- Mentally
- Physically
- Emotionally

By making your health a priority throughout the ups and downs of founding a company, you will be better positioned to achieve long-term success (and will ensure that you will be capable of being around for the long haul).

Maintaining personal health is the single best way to protect downside risk when starting a company.

TAKE CARE OF YOURSELF MENTALLY

When it comes to your mental space, I have come to believe you are what you eat. I have found that if I eat fast food, I tend to feel generally rotten and low in energy for the rest of the day. Likewise, I have noticed that if I consume trashy magazines, play video games, or zone out with too many reality TV shows, it's equivalent to filling my brain with junk food. My brain becomes sluggish and uncreative.

You might be saying to yourself how do I expect you to decompress? Don't get me wrong; it's absolutely important to unwind yourself from the pressures that come with founding a company, just as it's important to eat when you're hungry. But, like eating, you can choose things that will actually nourish you, or at least not zap your energy. Decompressing in a brain nourishing way instead of brain draining way. A great way to do that is to consume things that motivate and inspire you.

Read books that motivate, inspire, and help you be a better leader. There are great books I've read that are just as fun as trashy magazines, but packed with inspiration and health food for the brain. Try *Losing My Virginity* by Richard Branson, *The War of Art* by Stephen Pressfield, or anything by Seneca. Watch TED talks instead of playing video games. Listen to podcasts from people you admire instead of listening to news radio. If you put junk in, you're going to get junk out; but if you find inspiration, you're going to come up with things that you would never think of otherwise. Your lungs breathe even when you don't think about it. Your heart pumps without your help. Your brain is working on ideas and solutions even when you don't realize it.

Unconscious habits can also help or hinder mental health. For example, complaining is a common bad habit that eats away at your mental health. It is such an easy thing to do as the realities of startup life settle in, but it is toxic to your psychology. Complaining grows and spreads like a weed, and it will negatively impact you and those around you. In the history of mankind, complaining has never once created productive action, so you are far better off if you choose to be grateful.

A great mental habit is gratitude. I have found that gratitude happens to be a quick and easy way to counteract the urge to complain. Every time I have an urge to complain, I try to remember to look for something I'm grateful for instead. Are you grateful because you have a roof over your head? Are you grateful because you have a great spouse or partner? Are you grateful for the opportunity to build on your ideas? Put your focus there. Remember, nobody is pushing you to create a startup and nobody is forcing you to be stressed out all the time; you've imposed this on yourself. Resist the urge to complain and apply your energy to more productive pursuits, like feeding your brain.

TAKE CARE OF YOURSELF PHYSICALLY

A common and effective way to stay mentally healthy is to shut off your brain for a bit with exercise. Running, swimming, lifting weights, or other activities that punish the body will clear your mind. Even brisk walking can help. Maintaining good physical health through exercise and eating well does more than just giving your brain a break, your outer space is a reflection of your inner space. Good physical health allows your body to put its energy toward building your company. So take care of it.

This is especially important to remember when you're in the middle of a high-stress, high-pressure situation. People tend to make their worst decisions when coming from a place of fear and stress. Prioritize your physical health by blocking out regular times on your calendar for exercise, or even just going outside by setting a schedule and adhering to it.

What if you're scared of the gym or have a low self-image? These fears might be excuses that non-entrepreneurs can tell themselves, but if you are trying to do something extraordinary, you don't have the luxury of using these excuses. The stakes are too high and the pressure cooker situation will be prone to overtaking you. If you are not taking care of your physical body, you are a walking time bomb—not just for yourself and your company, but for your family and friends around you.

What if you don't want to pay for a gym membership? Running outside costs nothing. Or you can look up "How to Do a Burpee" on Google. Many consider burpees the single best all-around exercise you can do anytime anywhere with no equipment but your own body. It's the workout that prisoners use when they don't have access to weights. Alternatively, you can research the Scientific 7-Minute Workout on the New York Times website.

Jean-Paul Sartre said we don't choose to be born or die, but we choose everything in between. Nature gives us these bodies we inhabit, but it is up to us how well they are taken care of. If more people took half as much care of their own bodies as they do their cars or their house, we would all be better off for it. Our bodies are a present and we are all charged as the caregiver for a relatively short time on this planet.

TAKE CARE OF YOURSELF EMOTIONALLY

At this point, if you have already figured out how to take care of yourself mentally (reduce mental junk food and introduce more inspiration in your life) and physically (introduce a regular workout program in your life), you should pat yourself on the back. You are already doing more for yourself than most of the startup founders I know.

However, if you are not taking care of yourself emotionally, you are missing a critical part of keeping yourself in good shape for the long run. Building startups is an emotional rollercoaster. You might think you can manage your emotions without outside help, but chances are you are not as good at it as you think you are.

My advice to all founders is to get a therapist or a business coach. If you don't, you're missing out on a huge opportunity. You might wonder what a great business coach can tell you about your business since you are the domain expert. How much could they really know? In reality, it's one of the best things you can do for your business because it will help you avoid your own blind spots and emotionally driven decisions.

Emotional health often simply isn't prioritized in the same way as physical health. Even worse, no one really talks about it. Culturally, we seem to believe that seeing a professional to help you manage your emotional life is only necessary if something is very wrong. Mistakes like that can kill startups.

Mistakes come from having blind spots. The fact is, you are not objective when it comes to how you view your company. You have biases, expectations, and assumptions that can determine how you interpret events. For most people, the stakes aren't high enough for it to matter, but you are not most people. You are an entrepreneur. You can't afford to have blind spots.

You can't afford to be wrong because it can impact the future of your entire company. How do you see big mistakes when, by definition, you can't be objective? You have to have people who can watch your blind spots for you. Family and friends can help to an extent, but they bring their own baggage because they have a personal relationship with you.

When you only see where you choose to look, you're not getting the whole picture. In times like this, therapists or business coaches can provide a vital point of view. In addition to helping you manage your emotions, they are able to ask the questions that you're not asking yourself. They can view your decision-making processes objectively to help you determine whether you are making a choice from a reactive, emotional place when you should be approaching it differently. To choose not to seek outside help is to choose to disregard your emotional health and to ignore your blind spots. It's like driving without rear-view mirrors.

TECHNIQUE #2: PRACTICE REJECTION THERAPY

One of the biggest emotions many founders struggle with is fear of rejection. But rejection becomes a way of life when you're building a startup.

The natural human response to being told "no" is to feel upset. But when a founder begins fundraising and has to hear "no" from ninety-nine out of the a hundred investors he or she will talk to, that feeling can be overwhelming. If you don't think you are ready for high-volume rejection yet, you might give up prematurely. Your brain will be screaming, "Nope! I can't handle this anymore. No more trying. It's not worth it!" How do you find the strength to go on anyway?

No matter how great your idea is, most investors are likely going to think it's either a terrible idea or a great idea but not for them at this time. Silicon Valley is full of stories of successful entrepreneurs who were immediately rejected; every company you have ever heard of, including mine, was turned down by a lot of people. Some of the world's top-tier investors have blog posts about how they turned down Apple, eBay, Intel, and HP. Getting told "no" again and again is the reality of founding a company, and the sooner you can build resilience against it, the better off you'll be. The most effective way I've found to do this is to practice rejection therapy.

Rejection therapy is willingly subjecting yourself to being told "no" in order to build up a resistance to it. It's like lifting weights. It doesn't matter where you start, what matters is concerted effort over time. The more you do it, the more you will be able to tolerate and the stronger you become.

One of my favorite ideas comes from Noah Kagan's *How to Make a $1,000 a Month Business Course* from AppSumo. Next time you go to a coffee shop, ask for a ten percent discount. If it's a small coffee shop where you are a regular, maybe they'll give it to you. What's the downside risk? Then go to Starbucks, try the same thing, and see what happens. The point of the exercise is not about getting cheaper coffee; it's about asking for something, being prepared to hear no, and being okay with that. Sometimes you'll get it and sometimes you won't. In either scenario, you'll be actively learning how to deal with rejection.

There are so many other ways to practice rejection therapy. Try going up to somebody on the street and saying, "Can you give me five dollars?" Will you look like a bum? Maybe. Will you feel awkward? Definitely. How you look or feel isn't the point. The point is to get rejected. Subject yourself to uncomfortable situations to prove that you will come out on the other end unscathed.

Have fun with it (as much as you can) by getting creative. When you're in rejection therapy there are so many ways to look for rejection. There is even a website dedicated to it at **RejectionTherapy.com**. Make a list of ten ways you're going to get rejected during your day and check off each item as you go along. You can only fail if you don't look for ways to subject yourself to rejection.

By training yourself to withstand rejection, you will boost your confidence. You will no longer be beholden to your fear of being told "no." When you ask, "Can I please get a ten percent discount for that?" your voice will sound different. It will have a different tone to it. You will carry yourself differently. You will ask with a confidence that you didn't have when you were gripped in the icy hand of awkward fear. You will ask like someone who expects to hear "yes."

A great talent for any startup founder is to be immune to their emotional reactions. A great founder has no problem asking for something crazy, something completely out of this world, and if their request is rejected it doesn't bother them. That's not an accident and it's also not something they're born with. It must be learned. Rejection therapy is one of the really key ways to manage your own psychology, especially if you ever want to raise money.

TECHNIQUE #3: LEARN THE DIFFERENCE BETWEEN BIG PROBLEMS AND URGENT PROBLEMS

The best founders I know understand the difference between big problems and urgent problems. Urgent problems are immediate, important problems like raising investments, managing key customers, and dealing with troubled employees. Big problems can often feel urgent, but aren't. Some examples are preparing tax forms, figuring out how to set up payroll, and negotiating lease agreements. There is a huge difference between big problems and urgent problems. Fundamentally the difference comes down to is whether or not *you* need to be the person solving it.

Urgent problems shouldn't be delegated or outsourced. Hire people you can trust to take care of big problems and let yourself and your cofounders or leadership team focus on urgent problems. Life will be much easier if you let people do what they are good at by empowering them instead of micromanaging everything. Don't spin your wheels by spending your focus and energy on the details.

Here are some more urgent problems you should be thinking about:

- Do I have the right team to execute my idea?
- Do I have all the right people that can handle all the big problems?
- How can I get more big problems off my plate?
- Who can I trust to handle them appropriately?

When I learned to differentiate urgent problems from big ones, my day-to-day life became very different. It's so easy to move from one thing to another—putting out small fires as they continuously pop up—but when you do that, you get pulled into rabbit holes and can lose precious perspective on what actually needs your attention. Once you've lost perspective of the bigger picture, you are no longer thinking about the right things.

Think of yourself as the pilot of a passenger jet. Your job is to fly the plane and ensure safe delivery for everyone on board. If you are constantly trying to deal with problems that come up in the cabin—oh no! The guy in seat 37F really wants coffee and he's making a big fuss out of it!—you're much more likely to crash the plane or at least get lost. Whiny passengers and a lack of coffee are not the pilot's problem. Your job is to lead the plane to a safe destination.

One trick I found to help me snap out of small thinking was when I started working on a problem, I would habitually ask myself "How did this become a problem? Why does this problem exist? Is there something deeper going on?" After all, if you're not asking these questions, who will?

It can be difficult to resist the urge to solve every problem that arises when you have been the only one doing so for a while. As is so often the case in the early stages of building a company, there isn't anyone but you to resolve most problems. This can become a habit—into your very conception of what you think it means to be a founder—and it then feels unnatural to eventually put your trust into another person to handle the things you have had to manage for so long.

Another trick is to strategically not try to fix some problems. You have to be very careful selecting which problems you do this with, but I first noticed my own tendency to solve unnecessary problems one day while walking with my son.

I kept yelling for him to come back closer to me any time he strayed more than a few feet away. I realized that there might actually not be a causal link between my yelling and his realizing how far he strayed and coming back to me. So I stopped yelling. I stopped trying to obsessively intervene. My son would start to wander and I would hold my tongue. He would go one or two steps further than I felt comfortable, then, of his own accord, he would turn around and run back to hug my leg.

How many problems do you apply yourself to that would otherwise solve themselves if you stopped obsessively intervening? You can never know the answer if you don't start testing. There is no way to know for sure by hypothesizing.

Optimizing the types of problems I spent my time on changed the trajectory of my success and was one of the biggest things that set my successes apart from my failures.

TECHNIQUE #4: DEAL WITH THE MOST URGENT PROBLEM FIRST

I have a love-hate relationship with to-do lists, but I universally find that they are almost always being dramatically overused or underused. I have found a personal heuristic that has helped me get the most of to-do lists.

I find that the best time to start using a to-do list is the moment you recognize the stress or anxiety that you are going to forget something. Usually this is centered around a time-boxed project—that is, a project with a clear beginning and end. You shouldn't be carrying around any unnecessary stress as a startup founder because you will have plenty of things to stress about besides trying to remember things.

Any open-ended to-do list items that are not part of a time-boxed project tend to actually cause me stress instead of relieving it. Therefore, along the same line of logic to reduce stress, I do not keep to-do lists for things outside of time-boxed projects. Those lists only ever get bigger, until they become so long it can completely overwhelm you. This turns a productivity tool into an anti-productivity tool.

Instead, when you wake up in the morning, write down the single most urgent problem you need to solve—that is, what you have to tackle that day. Since you're only picking the single most urgent problem, you will be forced to think not only in terms of importance but also in terms of immediacy.

A great example of this was when 37Signals launched Basecamp. When Basecamp went live, the team realized they had not developed a way to accept payment for their service. It was a big problem, of course, but was it urgent? The company's founders decided it wasn't since the service was being given away for free on a thirty-day trial. This meant they didn't need to accept money for thirty days. They could focus their attention on other urgent problems in the early days of the launch. Accepting payment wasn't their most urgent problem until Day 29.

Start your day by asking yourself what your biggest, most urgent problem is. Is that your biggest problem? Is that really going to make or break your company today? Is it really that you don't have a corporate structure? Is figuring out how to minimize your taxes at the end of the fiscal year really your most urgent problem today? Is that going to make any difference to your bottom line? Answer these questions as objectively as you can and then get to work.

Any simple to-do list is invaluable when you are organizing

a complex event or a launch, or really anything that requires you to keep a lot of balls in the air for a short amount of time. When I do use a traditional to-do list, I select a date that is a couple days (or maybe one week) away and write it at the top of the list. This is the "throw away" date. When that day arrives, the list goes into the trash.

The fact is, as a founder, you shouldn't use to-do lists or other productivity tools like everyone else does. Once you allow yourself to trust those on your team to handle everything but urgent problems, you'll find that you don't really need one. Use your energy to keep a maniacal focus on the most urgent problems your startup is facing. By doing so, you'll resolve major issues and free up one of the most important resources a founder can have: time.

TECHNIQUE #5: PLACE A HIGH VALUE ON YOUR TIME

Time is one of the most precious commodities you have, and how you use your time is one of the biggest decisions you can make. It's crucial to the success of your startup that you know how to use your time effectively. As we discussed above, your time, energy, and focus should be reserved for solving urgent problems that arise in your company. But how do you determine where the rest of your time needs to go? One trick I've learned is to put a price on just how much your time is worth.

Several years ago, a good friend of mine gave me a piece of advice that has always helped me determine where and how to apply my time. He said, "Lucas, you're the CEO. Treat your time as being worth a thousand dollars an hour."

As an early startup founder, time is your most precious

asset—most likely far more valuable than you think. Try imagining your hourly rate as a thousand dollars and then act accordingly. Weigh everything on your plate against the value of your time. Should you be the person talking to the tax attorney if your time is worth a thousand dollars an hour? Should you be the one calling about a plumbing problem? The way that you treat your time will determine the actual value of your time. If you treat your time like it's worth eight dollars an hour, that's inevitably how other people will treat your time as well.

So if your time is worth a thousand dollars an hour, what activities are worth your rate? It is often activities that have the most upside and leverage. Here are some examples of activities that have more value than you may realize:

- Taking care of yourself
- Writing and storytelling
- Reflecting on urgent questions

Let's consider each of these activities in more detail and discover why they are so valuable.

TAKING CARE OF YOURSELF

Taking care of yourself is a highly leveraged activity. The quality of all your actions when you are in good physical, emotional, and mental health are all elevated. The quality of decisions and how you treat others is better too. One act with many various upsides is high leverage. The act of talking to a tax attorney when someone else can on your behalf has no leverage.

Founders often think they are far too busy to take time

for themselves. Their calendars are packed with back-to-back meetings and they are always behind on a major project. But calendars are often packed with eight dollars-an-hour tasks. Why does this happen? Because we let it happen.

Taking care of yourself physically, mentally, and emotionally is a thousand dollars-an-hour task. Therefore, it's probably more important than most of the things you feel so weighed down by. Strategize your schedule. If you eat and breathe by your calendar, use that to your advantage. Try scheduling time to take care of yourself directly into your calendar. Schedule yourself a massage. Schedule your workouts if you have to. Taking care of yourself is an investment easily worth over a thousand dollars an hour.

WRITING AND STORYTELLING

Telling stories is a highly leveraged activity. When you write—whether it is through your blog, website, or as an article contributor—you are creating content that will last forever and can be read hundreds or thousands of times. Write one blog post and one person reads it? Eight dollars an hour. One hundred people read it? Eight hundred dollars an hour. That's leverage.

Maybe you're thinking, "But what if I only reach ten people?" From a short-term perspective, you're absolutely right. If you approach writing from a long-term perspective, however, you will see that you are building a body of work. The content you write today will be something you can link to next year in support of another idea. It's something you can reference in a future article, and it's something that you can use to build relationships.

Not only is your writing an evergreen thing that will

live forever and be searchable on Google, it's also a creation process. In order to write, you need to think. You need to structure your ideas and communicate them in a way that makes sense outside of your own head. Through writing, you will practice talking about your company, product, or industry in a way that is very engaging and easy to connect to. And that's another incredibly valuable piece of leverage.

REFLECTING ON URGENT QUESTIONS

Possibly the most counterintuitive, highly leveraged activity is investing your time in quiet thought and reflection. People intuitively know that they get some of their best ideas in the shower, but then they don't shower more to have more good ideas.

Many founders are incredulous when I recommend they schedule quiet time on their calendar. When you're so accustomed to the fast pace and rigorous demands of building and leading a company, setting aside time for reflection can sound self-indulgent.

But this is the time to ask important questions, to think and create, and to weigh important decisions. And those are all things you need to do to steer your startup successfully. Taking time to reflect on a regular, if not daily, basis is an important thing you need to do as a leader. It is easily another thousand dollars-an-hour or even ten thousand dollars-an-hour activity because of what you might come up with if you let yourself.

Take twenty minutes each day to sit alone and undisturbed in your office. Go for a walk. Prioritize a small block of time to remove yourself from whatever is going on around you, and spend that time reflecting on what's going on, digesting what has already happened, and asking yourself questions that you don't usually ask. *Why am I doing this? Are there any urgent problems I'm missing?* If you don't prioritize this time in advance, it will never occur to you to do it at all. There's never a good time to say, "Oh boy, I think I'll take a meditation break." You'll never find yourself with nothing to do. You have to prioritize reflection and asking yourself urgent questions.

Always be aware that your time is highly valuable, and focus it accordingly. As the company founder, you can try prioritizing tasks by the leverage and optionality they afford you. And once you are in a position to pay other people to handle those small tasks, you can try to eliminate them altogether. Your focus belongs with the things that are worth your limited time, and with this strategy you can make sure it stays there. Take control of your own time, don't let your calendar control you.

TECHNIQUE #6: READ VORACIOUSLY

Reading is one of the best things you can do to maintain a healthy mental space. Whether you are learning something new, refining something you already know, or giving yourself space to be inspired, reading is vital to being a successful entrepreneur. And it's one of the first things most of us let fall by the wayside.

I'm guilty of thinking I was too busy to read. When I started AppFog I would make excuses. After a while, I finally realized that was just a story I was telling myself. Once I started reading again, I remembered how much value it brought to my life, and realized that allowing myself to fall out of the habit was one of the stupidest things that I had ever done.

Founders typically are really good at something—it's why they start their companies in the first place. However, building a successful company requires you to be actively involved in many facets of your business, not just the part you are good at. For example, a founder may be great at product or programming, but if he or she doesn't establish at least a base knowledge of sales and marketing there's going to be trouble ahead. Of course, you're going to hire people who are strong in those areas, but how will you lead them if you are completely unfamiliar with what they do? Your job isn't to be a sales or marketing expert, of course, but you need to learn enough to lead your team effectively.

There are so many things you don't know as an entrepreneur and reading is the best way to build the diverse knowledge base you need. Marketing, sales, business development, investing—these are all areas in which you need to build working knowledge. When it comes to fundraising in particular, there is a lot to be gained by learning the ins and outs of investors. There are so many great books about investing that will show you what investor psychology looks like; through books you'll understand what their strengths are, their hopes are, their weaknesses, why they ask certain questions. This is extremely valuable knowledge that can directly impact your startup. It is certainly worth your time.

Reading is a leveraged activity worth at least a thousand dollars an hour based on the ideas and decisions it could inspire. Warren Buffet, one of the best investors in the world, with an average twenty percent growth year-over-year (compared to the overall stock market of around twelve percent), spends eighty percent of his workday reading books. Reading is a way to have proximity to people you normally don't get access to. It's especially effective if you're reading about things that don't feed into your existing skill set. If you're naturally strong at creating products, use your time to learn about the areas you're unfamiliar with, like sales and marketing.

As a company founder, you have to become well rounded and competent enough to lead in every area of your company. That's an urgent problem that you need to start addressing now, especially when it comes to the things you can't eventually outsource to someone else. You should prioritize your focus on strengthening weaker skills.

TECHNIQUE #7: SURROUND YOURSELF WITH ADVISORS

Just like therapists and business coaches who can point out your emotional blind spots, business and startup advisors offer you much-needed business perspective on your company. Advisors can point out your business blind spots, offer their knowledge, support, and introductions to key individuals, and lend their experience to help you manage your organization and positively impact your company. They can also hold you accountable for metrics you want to hit like quarterly revenue or user growth goals. For this reason, one of the best things you can do is to surround yourself with advisors and communicate with them regularly.

Regular communication is the key to maintaining successful relationships. All too often, entrepreneurs make the mistake of allowing communication to drop for long spans of time, only to then reach out during a crisis. This is bad for both parties, as the founder is already in trouble and the advisor is brought into a mess he or she wasn't aware of. Seeking out your advisors only when something goes wrong is the worst way to manage these relationships.

Advisors are not people you go to when things go wrong, they are people you stay in touch with regularly. Whether it's through weekly email updates, bi-weekly phone calls, or monthly meetings, you need to be talking to your advisors on a regular basis. Weekly email updates promote a regular cadence of writing and reflection (two intrinsically valuable uses of your time). Get in the habit of sending a weekly update to every advisor you have, and you will see its benefits over the short and long term.

When updating your advisors, focus on reporting two things: cold hard numbers and your story.

Start with the numbers and make them completely objective: how many customers you signed up last week, what percentage of new that represents, how much revenue it is, etc. Numbers don't lie, and presenting them right up front will make you see exactly where you are as well. You can't bury your head in the sand when you're responsible for updating your numbers on a weekly basis. If you don't like what you see, then it's time to address it. Your advisor may be able to help you with it.

Then comes the story. "This week was a hard week. We had a difficult employee, and I had a talk with him about core values. If he does not improve I will have to let him go." The story is the second part of your update. Tell your advisors what went well and what went wrong. Tell them your biggest accomplishment of the week. Also, share the most urgent problem. Finally, ask for help.

If you're not asking for help every week, then you've got

a big blind spot. You cannot do everything—no matter what the mug on your desk says, you're not Superman. Ask for help and advice on a weekly basis.

By the time you realize that you're in crisis, you will have already been in crisis for a while. Most founders don't realize they're in trouble, that they're already beyond event horizon, until it's too late and things are going wrong. So if they're in regular contact with a team of advisors, small issues are more likely to be caught before they become urgent problems. Your advisors know you and they know your business without being completely immersed in it. If something is off, they are far more likely to see it before you do. It can be something as simple as an asynchronous thought in an email; sometimes it's your demeanor or the way you're behaving. If your advisors see something odd, they can warn you or ask probing questions. There are so few founders that utilize their advisors this way, and it is always to their own detriment.

Your advisors are available for more than just avoiding issues or managing problems. They are there for you to have a sounding board, something you constantly need. This's why it's valuable to choose a small group of people with very different perspectives and experiences. Look for people who have successfully raised money, who have successfully built companies, and those who have failed companies under their belts. Look for people with similar experience in similar and different industries. Diversify your advisory board.

As a founder navigating the high-pressure environment of building a company from the ground up, it can be very easy to find yourself overwhelmed by problems, projects, and demands on your time. Startup culture doesn't make your life any easier as the expectation is that you have spent years grinding out your work in twenty-hour days, sacrificing your health and personal relationships in the name of keeping your business running.

Recognize that your time and attention is extremely valuable. Act like it too. Use that as a tool to determine where your focus needs to be. Solve the issues that are creating your biggest problems and let someone else solve the other problems. Or let those problems solve themselves. When you let a problem solve itself, you don't just ignore it or pretend it isn't there. You watch it and keep tabs on it, but choose not to intervene. After all, there may come a point where it is critical you do take action. If my son did run into the street, I would need to be ready to run after him.

Prioritize your self-care, self-improvement, and personal accountability. These are the things that truly matter and the areas in which you will benefit your startup and your team the best. It may be difficult initially to phase yourself out of eight dollars-an-hour tasks and trusting someone else to put out small fires but the adjustment is well worth it. The founder's psychology is focused on the big picture—on strategy, leadership, and the relationships that will grow your business.

The Logistics of Building a Startup

The Internet is full of logistical advice about how to create a startup, but most of it is in piecemeal random blog posts that mostly conflict with each other. When I started out, I would try to search for things like "how to incorporate in Delaware" and "what's the difference between an LLC and an S corporation?" I would try to make the best decisions I could, but I often felt blind to the bigger picture and how it all fit together. I wished a fellow entrepreneur would save me time and just step through the important logistics in the right order and tell me what was normal for most startups. So now I would like to do that for you so that you can find success in my failures.

If you have done a few startups already and spent time learning all about startup logistics, this chapter might be review. Still, I encourage you to skim through it anyhow. There may be a few ways of looking at things here that you hadn't thought of before. If you haven't gone through the process yet, hopefully this chapter can clarify and streamline you so that you can spend more time delighting your customers.

Startup logistics are hard. Separating the important decisions from the urgent ones takes experience and wisdom. After I'd spent a long day negotiating a particularly tricky business deal, my wife once asked me: "What do you want to do tonight, eat out or stay in?"

I just stared at her blankly. I was paralyzed. It was like I had a certain number of decisions in me for the day, and they had all been used up. I was decision bankrupt.

The decisions you make for your company often have long-term consequences. As a founder, your job literally consists of making a lot of decisions quickly. And especially when you're in the early stages of your business, you rarely have enough time or information to make informed decisions.

I often found the pressure to make all these decisions overwhelming. The sheer volume of logistical and strategic decisions that need to be made and the implication those choices can have on your future has led many founders to anxiety, panic attacks, and worse.

There are many ways founders manage these feelings. One of the most common is simply to avoid making decisions altogether.

Founders who want to avoid making decisions, or doing the real hard work of the day, can come up with an endless array of excuses. I used to tell myself I needed more time to make a decision, or I needed more information, or better information. Or better yet, I would obsess about things like my bank account (or lack thereof), the latest news, the stock market, cat photos, Facebook stalking. We all have a comforting set of rabbit holes that let us spin our wheels and spend energy ineffectively.

Decisions still need to be made, and instead of waiting for perfect confidence in any one decision, I have learned to act on my best judgment and pick up the pieces later. For particularly important decisions, like legal and accounting matters, I hire experts to offer an array of choices and lay out the pros and cons of each. Then I act and pick up the pieces later.

Decision making for an entrepreneur can be daunting. If you make quality decisions early on, you are setting yourself up for success. If you make the poor decisions, they can create unnecessary headaches and potentially threaten the entire business down the line.

One of the first decisions you make as an entrepreneur is to start a company in the first place. Even this decision can be fraught with rabbit holes: "Do I register as an LLC? Would an S corp be a smarter choice than a C corp? In what state should I register my corporation?"

You can spend endless hours pounding these questions into search engines and spinning your wheels, but these are not where you should be spending your time as an entrepreneur. You need to spend your time talking to customers, understanding their pains, and building great products. You don't need to be a great lawyer on top of everything else you bring to the table, so stop trying. Go pay a great lawyer and accountant to clear a path for you. To not do this is penny-wise, pound-foolish. Most importantly, it's a waste of your most precious asset: your time.

In general, I have discovered some guiding principles to making good decisions. If I follow these principles, it usually keeps me out of trouble. It's like a decision-making bumper lane. Even if I don't always make the best decisions, these principles make it easier to clean up my messes down the road.

1. PROTECT THE DOWNSIDE
   Richard Branson when starting his Virgin Airlines made a deal while leasing airplanes from Boeing that at any time he could return them and the lease would be canceled without penalty. That's classic downside protection. When evaluating a decision, spend time evaluating the ways it could go wrong, because the upside can take care of itself.

2. ALWAYS MAINTAIN YOUR LONG-TERM OBJECTIVE PERSPECTIVE
   No deal is ever a "must-do" deal. Walking away is always a decision available to you in any situation. Getting caught up in the moment, whether from excitement or anger or fear is a surefire way to make bad decisions. Good decisions always come from a place of logic and perspective.

3. NEVER LET ANYONE ELSE MAKE IMPORTANT DECISIONS FOR YOU
   Especially people you pay on an hourly basis. Others can give you perspective and advice, but handing them the keys is never a good idea. You can only delegate decision making to fully committed team members who are held responsible for those decisions.

4. OPEN THE LINES OF CLEAR, HONEST COMMUNICATION
   Start with yourself. Throughout the startup experience, honesty with yourself and others is key to good decision making. There will be tough decisions to be made with your cofounders, employees, spouse, friends, and even lawyers. Good decisions often can't come in these situations without full disclosure.

DIFFICULT CONVERSATIONS

In my experience, some of those early honest conversations were the most difficult but critical to have. It's a matter of saying everything you need to say to the other person now, so that if something bad happens down the road there will already be a plan in place.

It requires absolute honesty and a willingness to discuss your company in a very frank way, which can make these conversations scary. Still, it's better to put everything on the table in advance with the people you respect: your cofounder, your spouse, and your boss. We will discuss each of these kinds of conversations one by one.

COFOUNDERS AND EARLY EMPLOYEES

Bringing on cofounders and hiring early employees can be thrilling and exciting, but before jumping into these long-term relationships you should get to know each other as quickly and intimately as possible. Here are some of the tough conversations I have had over and over again:

- Why are we doing this?
- What are our desired outcomes (early exit, IPO, lifestyle business, etc.)?
- Who is responsible for what?
- What are our compensation expectations (equity, salary, benefits, etc.)?
- How will we make decisions when we can't agree?
- What will we do if we run out of money?

- Are our core values aligned?
- Where do we stand on using our personal networks?

None of these questions should be taken for granted. Even if you think you know the answers. Maybe you think they are obvious. Until it is codified into a signed agreement, even if it is a non-binding document of understanding, nothing is as obvious at it seems.

Let's dig into a few of these questions in more depth.

WHO IS RESPONSIBLE FOR WHAT?

Fights tend to happen when two people want the same thing, not when they want different things. If my product manager and sales guy both think they are responsible for marketing, they are not going to get along. Setting clear boundaries is hard in a startup, because people have to wear multiple hats, but keeping the lines as clear as possible is critical for a healthy culture.

Cofounders should determine exactly what the individual roles and responsibilities will be up front. All too often, these things will go unsaid because it seems intuitive, particularly when one or both of you is naturally suited for a particular role (one is more technical, the other is more business-savvy, etc.) While it may feel like it's a natural split, if you don't know who the official CEO is, for example, then you need to figure it out sooner rather than later. Make sure all of you are on the same page.

- Who is going to be the public face of the company (talk to press and analysts)?
- Who's the CEO?

- What does CEO mean to us?
- Who is in charge of building and maintaining which relationships (customers, investors, advisors)?
- Who is the better presenter and to which people (conferences, events, fundraising)?

Once you have determined your respective titles, you must agree on the roles and responsibilities of each one. Be very thorough and very explicit—leave no detail unexamined. This exercise should be fractal. It starts with the founders, who do it with their executive team, who should do it with their teams, and so on down the line.

COMPENSATION EXPECTATIONS

It may seem obvious to say things like equity and compensation must be discussed between you and your cofounders. And for some, maybe it is. But I know of many examples in which these important questions were taken for granted.

In one instance, I was speaking to a friend of mine, another founder in the beginning stages of building his company. As he talked, I could sense that he had missed some seemingly obvious discussion points with his cofounder. Then he said, "We're about to go fundraising."

"Okay," I said. "What's your equity split?"

"Well, we don't have anything written down yet, but we're *obviously* going to split it in half."

"Hold on, that's not obvious at all," said his cofounder.

An even equity split is common, and perhaps even assumed for startup teams. But it may not be the best structure for your partnership. For example, what if the first founder had been working on the startup for a year or two before the second founder came along? Or what if one of the founders brings a huge advantage to the business? Or what if one founder can put more time into the project than the other?

If one person quits their job to dedicate all their time to the startup, while the other stays at their job and dedicates their nights, it is not an equitable split of their time. An uneven division might not justify an even divide of the company.

The secret to figuring out equity split is that there is no secret. Every situation is unique. But the biggest troubles with determining equity come when cofounders do not bring honesty and respect into the conversation. Remember that you plan to work with these people for the next five to ten years, if not the rest of your career. Everyone should be slightly uncomfortable with the end result, but nobody should feel taken advantage of.

It may take a long time to reach the point that you can afford to take a salary, but you must determine your salary terms at the very beginning. Talk to each other about your salary expectations. Some important questions to ask are:

- What's the equity split?
- How much do you each expect to get paid?
- At what point will you each get paid?
- How long can you live without getting paid?
- If one person needs the money and one person doesn't, how does that affect the equity split?

HOW DO YOU MAKE DECISIONS WHEN YOU CAN'T AGREE?
It is unlikely that the two of you will agree on every decision you will need to make for your company. Disagreements can be fine, provided that you have a plan in place to resolve them.

Talk to your cofounder to determine how you will make decisions when you don't agree on what the outcome should be:

- Does the CEO get final say?
- Do you flip a coin?
- Do major stockholders have to vote?
- What's the definition of a major stockholder?

A good lawyer can help you think through these questions and even give you common solutions others have found.

Important Note: You can't determine your mutual decision-making process when you're in the middle of a disagreement or a fight. You have to think about those kinds of things *before* they happen.

WHAT TO DO IF YOU RUN OUT OF MONEY

Don't make the mistake of not preparing for what will happen if everything goes wrong. If you turn to your partner in three months and say, "I haven't had any income for months. I can't do this anymore. I have to go get a job," it's a huge problem. Blindsiding your partner will burn bridges and hurt your reputation.

Discussing worst-case scenarios up front may be unpleasant, but it's essential. Talk to your cofounder about what you will do if things go very badly:

- How long can you last without getting paid?
- How long can your cofounder last without getting paid?
- What will you do if you can't raise money?

Protect your downside. Develop plans for each of these scenarios. Then, if the worst should happen, you each already know what is going to happen. You already talked about it. Once you have developed your plan, stick to it.

ARE YOUR CORE VALUES ALIGNED?
Just like determining your own core values, it's important to determine your shared core values with your cofounders.

Bring your core values to the table as a team, discuss them openly, and ensure that they are aligned. If you don't agree with your cofounders on what those core values are, or if your values conflict, then you need to seriously consider whether to move forward with the partnership.

These conversations aren't easy to have. Sometimes it can be very unpleasant. But the consequences of avoiding these tough discussions with your cofounder are far worse. All of these questions are so essential and, if you haven't discussed them up front, could ultimately result in a company-ending fight or a ruined relationship.

- What's the company's mission and purpose for its customers?
- What are the basic principles we all believe in?
- Are there a few key rules that can't ever be broken?
- What kind of work environment do we want to nurture?

SPOUSE/SIGNIFICANT OTHER

My wife was six months pregnant when I quit my job to start AppFog. One of the biggest mistakes a lot of founders make is keeping their spouses or significant others on the outside. They have all this turmoil going on inside their heart and their mind and their head—they're scared—but instead of talking about it with their partners they hold it in.

The reality in my experience was that often my wife was just as scared as I was. If I had told her "Oh, everything's going to be great. Funding won't be a problem and I will have a salary again in no time," not only would she have not believed it, she would have felt alienated and alone with her fears.

The most important part of keeping a relationship together through a startup is staying on the same team. You can't force your significant other to be on your team, and there will be times when you might feel like they are not on your team. This hurts a lot when it happens. After all, if you are like me, then a big part of why you are taking this risk is to secure your family's financial future.

Being on the same team isn't a logical thing based on reasoned thinking. It's about being on the same emotional team. And that means you have to always be honest about your emotions: good, bad, and ugly. If you aren't letting your spouse in, how do you expect them to stay on your team?

Maybe you think your significant other won't understand, or worse that they won't care. Maybe you are worried about what they will say when you tell them about the risks. It can feel much easier to bury your head in the sand and gloss over everything. Pulling back the curtain and letting them see what's going on can be scary. But if you didn't want to do this, you shouldn't have started a company. This process is brutal. And it's brutal for them too. Being the spouse of a startup founder is hard. Acknowledge that and show gratitude. They might know it's for a family legacy, but sometimes that's not enough.

The primary aim of these conversations is to honestly inform. You will need to discuss:

- How much time and money will (realistically) be invested?
- How much travel and time away from home is acceptable?
- What are the risks and realistic outcomes?
- Will your partner give you honest feedback or be your undying cheerleader?
- Which one would you like them to be?
- Which one are they comfortable being for you?

The fact is startups tear many relationships apart, no matter how strong they may be. Honest communication is essential, not just in these initial conversations but also throughout the entire process. It is essential that you are able to tell the truth to—and hear the truth from—your partner.

WHAT ARE THE RISKS AND REALISTIC OUTCOMES?

I've talked to lots of founders that are really scared of sitting down with their spouse to discuss what might go wrong. And often the spouse is even *more* scared of this conversation!

Lots of startups fail; it's very common for them to fail. When people say that nine in ten startups fail, everyone thinks they are the one exception. The nine failures aren't all bad companies. You will hear about them in the press raising tens of millions of dollars. Many startups you would never expect to fail end up failing. Even companies that get acquired can be failures. Companies can be sold for less money than investors put in and the employees end up without a thing. This happens more often than people like to admit.

Explaining how startups work to your significant other

is an essential part of maintaining a strong bond. Again, you have to be realistic about what could happen and what is possibly very likely to happen. Give your spouse a clear picture of what to expect and set the tone for honest communication in your relationship. They should know that the overwhelming likelihood is that your startup will fail.

Invest and prioritize this kind of honest communication, especially during the hard parts. Put a lot of care and thought into keeping your spouse up to date with everything that is going on. You can't just forget about it, you can't just sweep it under the covers.

This is a difficult conversation, and an ongoing one.

HOW MUCH TIME AND MONEY WILL BE INVESTED?

You have an obligation to be honest and transparent about how much money is being spent, how it is being spent, and where it is going, especially if you're married.

If you haven't done it before, asking for money, or for permission to spend it, can be very daunting. It can be an emotionally difficult thing to do. Unfortunately, you're going to have to do it a lot, both to customers and investors. With investors, it's very likely that you will have to talk up to a hundred investors before you get anybody to sign you a check. So do yourself a favor and start building up resistance to the discomfort of asking for money now.

Instead of feeling scared about discussing the time and monetary investment with your spouse, use it as practice for building resistance to the discomfort of money. Sit them down and say: "Here's why I think we should spend five hundred dollars on a designer for our homepage."

Your spouse/significant other will likely respond with the

same sort of questions you will get from investors:

- *"Wow that's a lot of money, can we afford to do this?"*
- *"Why are we spending it?"*
- *"Do we really have to spend it now?"*

Depending on how familiar your significant other is with the process, you might have to counteract a lot of skepticism—perhaps even more so than you would with a seasoned investor who really understands what's going on. Whether it is a spouse or an investor, if you aren't prepared to make your case you probably won't get the answer you want.

WILL YOUR SIGNIFICANT OTHER GIVE YOU HONEST FEEDBACK?

When I first run ideas by my friends, the response I hear most frequently is: "Oh yeah, that sounds good."

It's easier to say an idea sounds good than to say it's stupid. My friends don't want to make me feel bad, after all. Neither do yours.

My wife, on the other hand, calls me on my bullshit ideas. She will not fall for every crazy, harebrained idea that I have. The perfect friend or significant other to have in this situation is someone who can be brutally honest with you. If your idea is bad, they will tell you. If you have a problem, they will tell you. And you need that. You need someone who can help you think through problems, not someone who will just say "yes." It is your responsibility to involve your spouse/partner and make them your first and primary and most important trusted adviser.

There is an old saying: "When it comes to breakfast, the

chicken is involved, but the pig is committed." Who's committed in your life? Are you really treating them that way?

YOUR BOSS

For years, I wanted the upside of a startup without any of the downside risk. I thought, *I can do a startup on the side. I'll run it as a side business, and if it takes off I can raise money. And once I raise money, I'll quit my job and everything will be fine.*

If you watch ABC's Shark Tank, you know one of the first questions that savvy investors pose to entrepreneurs is "Are you doing this full time?"

When the answer is no, it is a part-time, side business, the chances of investment (both inside and outside of the Shark Tank) plummet. There are very few exceptions. Many entrepreneurs hope to raise money primarily so they can afford to pay themselves and quit their current jobs. Unfortunately, investing in unproven ideas so that the founder can take a salary is one of the biggest turn-offs for investors.

Leaving the security of your job can be one of the scariest parts of starting a company. And you can't get around it, so stop trying.

Having an honest conversation with your boss is an important part of the process too. It is important that you don't burn that bridge. To do so may be a short-term gain (maybe you hate him and want to tell him what you really think), but it's very bad practice in the long term. Who do you think professional investors are going to call as a reference?

Professional investors never ask you for references, they do their background checks without asking you. They look into your history and they reach out through their own networks to get to your boss. They know not to trust you, because they can't afford to be wrong. They're writing you checks for millions of dollars. They're not going to just say, "Oh, the three references you listed sound pretty good, I'll call those people." They need to know the truth about you—the real truth—so they do all the research on their own.

There are no hacks. There are no shortcuts. Your relationship with your boss is a bridge you can rarely afford to burn.

When you talk to your boss, you don't need to lay out everything like you would with your significant other. You have to be mindful of intellectual property concerns. There are some things that you should disclose and other things that you don't need to.

For example, you should make it clear that you're using your own personal time and your own personal resources to build your company. You're not using their office or printer ink or anything like that. If you have any hesitations about this conversation at all, talk to your lawyer.

It's also great if you can summarize the verbal conversations in an email or a letter. A written paper trail where your boss acknowledges that he does not believe you are infringing company intellectual property or using their time or resources can be hard to get, but very valuable for the diligence process when raising money.

These are the essential conversations to have before you move on to logistical matters. Yes, they're difficult. That's why it's best to get them off your plate. More importantly, you're starting this journey in a respectful way—one that is likely in line with your core values. By establishing open, honest communication with your cofounder and your spouse, you're setting the tone for what you can each expect from the other as you weather the ups and downs of building a company. By maintaining a positive relationship with your boss, you will ensure that you depart from your current job honorably and without burning any bridges.

Now, it's time to move into the logistics of setting up your company. I have broken them up into One-Time Tasks and Recurring Tasks.

ONE-TIME TASKS

PICK A NAME

I find that picking the perfect name for my businesses can be a very stressful, difficult process that I have done wrong many times.

Because naming a company can be very personal and very subjective, there isn't a lot of good advice for choosing a name. There are, however, some important "Dos" and "Don'ts" that I have learned over the years. For example:

DO spend a lot of the time writing a list of ideas and show them to friends and trusted advisers to see what sounds good and what doesn't. Use people you trust as a sounding board, and take their feedback seriously.

DON'T box yourself into a niche by choosing a highly specific name. This can make it difficult for you if you decide to extend in a new direction in the future.

I made this mistake when I started AppFog.

AppFog was originally called PHP Fog, and at the time I thought it was perfect. *Well, I thought, this is a PHP technology company, and I want people to know that, so I'm just going to call it PHP.* Naturally, it took less than a year for me to realize I wanted to do more than PHP. But I had boxed myself in with my company's name.

I spent a year trying to rename the company. It took a very long time and it was very expensive. Renaming a company is something I wouldn't wish on any founder.

DON'T pay attention to naming trends. Adhering to a naming trend can be as binding as an overly specific name. Trends come and go, and when the naming trend you choose to follow falls by the wayside (and it will) you will be stuck with a company name that timestamps you in the past.

DON'T pick a name that is hard to spell or pronounce. If your company's name is hard to spell then people are going to misspell it. If a potential customer types your company's name into their web browser incorrectly, they're not going to find you; and it won't take too many missed attempts before they're going to stop trying. Similarly, don't choose a name that is hard to pronounce. If your company's name is a mouthful, you're going to be at a disadvantage for word of mouth sharing. And word of mouth is an incredibly important part of spreading startups.

In *Contagious: Why Things Catch On*, Jonah Berger studied the effectiveness of word of mouth sharing online versus offline. He found that only seven percent of word of mouth happens online. Face-to-face sharing trumps Facebook by over ninety percent! So if you make your company's name hard to pronounce, you're making your company hard to share.

DO remember, when nobody knows you exist, the last thing you want is to be hard to find or hard to talk about.

Domain names are another important matter of consideration and carry a set of "Dos" and "Don'ts" as well:

DO be flexible when selecting a domain name. A lot of people think their domain names have to be really focused.

They think, *Well, I can't buy fubar.com so I have to pick a different name.* This isn't the case at all. You have a lot of flexibility in the exact domain name that you pick. Once you find a name for your company that you really believe in, don't let the domain name availability dictate whether or not you move forward with it. "Getfubar.com" is not going to ruin your chances of people finding your site.

DO a trademark search. Choosing a name that has already been protected by someone else is another great way to box yourself in. You can do an initial search on your own, but my advice is to reach out to your lawyer for assistance.

DO try to think of a name you can visualize. If your company's name can create a picture in your customer's head, in their mind's eye, it will solidify the association. MailChimp, for example, is a great visual name because you can just imagine this little chimp with a mailman's hat. It makes the name memorable. If you can help people see in their head what that name means, then they will remember your name.

DO draw upon associations to convey what you do. When I started Craftsman Founder, I wanted a name that communicated my long-term perspective on startups. By drawing on the associations and imagery a craftsman conveys—artistry, skill, experience, dedication—I am able to give people a sense of what Craftsman Founder is without a follow-up explanation. You can do this in other ways too; you don't have to be as direct and you can be a little bit clever. Turn to other languages for inspiration, create an inside joke that your customers will get. Choose something symbolic and meaningful.

DO seek out and listen carefully to negative feedback. When I started PHP Fog, there were very few people that told me it was a bad name; but a few did. I didn't listen to them. I wrote off their criticism and found ways to justify it to myself. In retrospect, they were absolutely right. You have to surround yourself with people that are willing to be really honest with you, but you also have to listen to them carefully.

Selecting a name for your company is a craft—another instance in which long-term thinking is essential. It may take a long time before you find a name that makes sense, one that is meaningful to you and effectively communicates what your company is. Think of that time as a long-term investment and don't rush the process.

Otherwise you'll end up with a name like PHP Fog.

Task Review:

- Pick a name (free)
- Register a domain name with NameCheap or Gandhi ($10/year)
- Set up a business email account with FastMail or Google Apps ($10-50/year)
- Save all the receipts to Evernote or Dropbox

PICK A BUSINESS STRUCTURE

There are a lot of details that founders can become obsessed with, and this tends to be one of the big ones. Instead of focusing on the target customer and hair-on-fire problems, a lot of founders will dedicate their time and energy to *What kind of business structure do I use? LLC? C corp? S corp? B corp?* It's understandable, because once you pick a structure it's not easy to move to a different one. I know because I've set up—and had to change—many of them.

I've set up every kind of structure there is. I've done it

using the online legal forms (something I will never do again) and I've done it using lawyers. It's something I've done many times, and if you plan on being a craftsman of startups, it's something you're going to do many times too. If you're going to build businesses, chances are that you are not likely to create just one or two, you're likely to create a bunch of them. And most of them will fail.

Whether it's your first company, or your fifteenth, it's always important that you incorporate. When I was starting my first company, I set up an LLC. I thought, *I don't want to go through the rigmarole of a C corporation,* because there is a lot of procedural stuff that goes along with that. But I wanted something really official sounding. I wanted the pride that came with holding a legal entity.

An LLC seemed like the way to go, but I was ignoring a crucial fact: I was a sole proprietor. I didn't have cofounders at the time, it was just me. Without a cofounder and with few valuable assets to your name, an LLC makes little sense. The biggest advantage is liability protection; but I didn't have assets worth suing for, nor did my business make enough money to be worth anything. So the liability was not worth protecting.

Sole-proprietorships involve much less paperwork, are far less in fees, and are incredibly easy to set up. An LLC on the other hand has extra paperwork and fees. You have to pay your state, pay the registration fees, pay your taxes, and it can quickly add up to hundreds or thousands of dollars that must be paid on a yearly basis. If you're not making any money yet, extra expenditure is the last thing you want. Shutting down an LLC can be a hassle too.

If you don't have any cofounders and don't have much

money yet, you should consider skipping the LLC completely. Go with a sole-proprietorship instead. It's much less work and you can still get the pass-through tax benefits at the end of the year if you keep a separate bank account and receipts.

If you have multiple cofounders, just set up a C corp with a lawyer. It is as simple as that. Don't even spend time thinking about it. Once you're ready to quit your job or raise money, or you're getting serious, getting significant revenue, then you will already have setup the correct corporate structure. Keep it simple for as long as you can. Don't try to do anything funny; don't try to reinvent the wheel.

And when you are ready to move into a C corp from a sole proprietorship (in order to add founders, advisors or investors), call a lawyer.

It is very easy for a good lawyer to convert your company's structure when the time is right. You can simply walk into your lawyer's office and say, "I have a sole-proprietorship, I need a C corp." That's bread and butter for them; it's very easy and relatively inexpensive for them to do. On the other hand, it can be very hard for you to do on your own. This is why you don't want to set up a C corp up front. Establishing a C corp up front is a big headache; C corps cause a lot of pain, their fees eat up a lot of money, and it takes a lot of time. Don't waste your time when lawyers are set up to do that for you. Once you go to the lawyer, they will easily set everything up, transfer all the assets, and they will do it the right way.

As a startup founder, your job isn't filling out boring paperwork. Your job is figuring out *How do I create something that adds value to people's lives?* If you are happy to dedicate your time to figuring out the corporate legal bylines, if that's what you really obsess about and are passionate about, you might be better off going to law school instead of starting a company. Companies are for creating business value, and that's where the founder's focus belongs.

A founder's job is to think about the big problems and devise solutions, to figure out the company's direction, and to be a leader. A founder is not the person who obsesses about every line in every single legal document. As a founder and CEO, it's your job to lead the company. There is a big difference between leadership and execution. You should be hiring people to execute on the direction that you're setting.

Managing Your Predisposition to Delay Decisions

These early decisions critically rely on your ability to manage your mentality while you're going through this process. So many of these steps are really great opportunities for a founder to delay decisions, especially if overwhelmed with fear. So how do you combat the temptation to hem and haw over these foundational logistics?

There are multiple things you have to do. First, you have to realize that this is a common tendency and learn to recognize it within yourself. If you recognize certain things that you tend to do when you're stressed, if you know yourself well enough—that you know you go into rat holes—then you can start looking out for that. If you know the kinds of traps you easily fall down, that will help too. The good news is that once you know what to look for, it becomes much easier to fight back. It's simply a matter of finding the solutions that work best for you.

One way you can do this is by relying on your relationship with your significant other, or someone who knows you well. Ask them to help you snap out of a rut by saying, "I know that

I can get obsessed about stupid stuff sometimes, can you tell me when I'm currently obsessing about something stupid?" What good friend wouldn't jump on an open invitation to call you out? People usually won't call you out unless you explicitly give them permission. If you give them permission, it makes it easier for everyone. With permission, your significant other won't feel like they're nagging you, they'll feel like they have an active participation role.

By pro-actively asking for constructive criticism, you are also creating a system to manage your blind spots. You are recognizing that you have weaknesses, and sometimes get scared and run into rat holes. Instead of living in denial, you are creating an environment that helps you succeed despite your own shortcomings.

By creating systems to manage your own shortcomings, you are acting like Homer's hero Odysseus in the Odyssey. Odysseus has his men tie him to the boat's mast and fills their ears with wax so that he can safely listen to the Sirens' song without being seduced into crashing himself into the rocks. Like Odysseus, you have to find ways to tie yourself to the mast. You have to figure out ways that you can make up for your weaknesses. This is just one example, and it might not work for everyone. If you have people you can trust, you can create all kinds of checks and balances with them to prevent you from crashing into rocks.

Sometimes it might just be that you've slipped into auto-pilot and you don't even know you're obsessing. You could spend days digging into things without even realizing it. You need to establish systems that keep you from wasting your time.

After all, the only asset you really have as a startup in these early stages is time. You don't have money, you don't have people, you don't have employees, you don't have much; the only thing you have is time. Time is your only currency. And even with time, you don't have much of it. You only have as much as will last until you go bankrupt.

So you must use your time wisely. You have to deploy it carefully. Like your last canteen of water, you can't waste it. Your only chance at success in business is if you can take whatever small amount of time you have to dedicate yourself to your company and turn that into revenue. Companies are for creating business value, and that's where the founder's focus belongs.

Task Review:

- Pick a legal structure ($25–$500)
- Register with the IRS to get an EIN Tax ID, a social security number for your business (free)
- Save your receipts to Evernote or Dropbox

OPEN A BANK ACCOUNT

Time may be your only currency, but you still need to open a bank account. And it is not that hard.

Opening a bank account may sound like a menial administrative task, but it is one of those things you shouldn't skip. Founders that do not open their own business account, do it at their own peril. From a long-term perspective, it always makes sense for your businesses to have their own bank accounts from the start. The good news is, it's a lot easier to set up a bank account than you might think it is, and it takes very little time. Simply bring the registration forms for your C corp, LLC, or sole-proprietorship, and the bank will do the rest.

Once your account is set up, it's very important that everything you spend comes out of the company bank account and that you keep all your receipts.

Everything you do, whether you are receiving or paying people money, or paying for equipment and software, all of that needs to happen within your company bank account. Do not neglect this, or occasionally pay from other sources. It will be an unnecessary nightmare if you don't keep all payments from a single corporate source. You're going to have to go back and spend lots of time sorting through your personal purchases and separating out your business expenses. You don't want to have to do that. Avoid all of that headache by setting up a bank account up front. It's not worth skipping this step.

Task Review:

- Open a checking account (free)
- Open a credit card (free)
- Save your banking documents to Evernote or Dropbox

RECURRING TASKS

These are the tasks that will be ever present as you build your company. Prioritize these tasks early on, devise an efficient way to stay on top of them, and you will greatly benefit your business over the long term.

EVERNOTE & QUICKBOOKS

Just as you'll want to establish your company bank account right from the start, you also want to save and organize your receipts. Your future self will thank you. This task may be easier for some than it is for others.

Some people are naturally nit-picky when it comes to saving their receipts. They'll keep every receipt for everything, even the hamburger that they bought at McDonald's in January. Why? You're not going to return your hamburger; why do you need to keep your hamburger receipt? Are you going to claim it as a business expense? Unless you are actually entertaining customers at McDonald's, then you are cheating the tax man, and nobody can cheat the tax man forever.

I sit on the other end of the spectrum: I hate receipts. I do not like them anywhere near me, and for years I started businesses and never kept a single receipt. It took my first audit to cure me of that behavior forever.

You want to strike a balance between being a receipt hoarder and a receipt tosser.

When I first started keeping receipts, I would just throw them into a folder. That's better than not having them at all, but you are creating a future headache for yourself.

Discovering Evernote finally enabled me to really successfully organize my receipts and save my sanity. With Evernote (or Dropbox or Box.net), I can take and sync pictures of receipts and immediately throw away the physical copy. By saving digital copies, I can keep records for as long as necessary and easily retrieve what I need when I need it.

Why do I use Evernote instead of Dropbox or Box.net? Search. Evernote has built-in text recognition for every picture taken. Once a receipt is uploaded, you can search for it.

So the $2.34 spend that you made three years ago? You can type "2.34" in Evernote and it will match it up to the correct receipt in seconds.

It takes a few seconds to take a picture before throwing the receipt away. This is the digital equivalent of throwing them into a folder, but making it searchable helps you in the long term. At some point, you're going to hire people who need all those receipts, and when that time comes you can just hand them your Evernote account and say, "There they all are."

You have no idea how much time, money, and how many headaches you will save yourself by keeping everything filed from the beginning. Do it, no matter how much you hate receipts.

In addition to saving receipts, get in the habit of saving every other important document into Evernote, Dropbox, Box. net, or something similar. The legal registration, tax registration and forms, insurance paperwork. Use Evernote, Dropbox, or Box.net as your dumping ground.

By the way, getting a Tax ID for your company is super simple. You just go to **http://j.mp/ein-registration**, type in your company's name, and they give you an EIN (like a social security number for companies) on the spot. Keep that document in Evernote, Dropbox, or Box.net, of course.

Then do yourself another huge favor and set up Quick-Books from the beginning. Do it as soon as you set up your company bank account. Link your QuickBooks account to your bank account so that it immediately starts to import your transactions into QuickBooks. Treat your business like a business. It is incredibly important that you do this from the beginning, even before you are making money. Set yourself up for success, knowing that you will eventually hire an accountant to make sense of it all for you. Maintaining your QuickBooks from the beginning will make your accountant's life easier too.

Save your receipts. Utilize Evernote, Dropbox, or Box.net. Set up QuickBooks. Save your documents. These are all little habits that will make a huge impact down the road.

Task Review:

- Download QuickBooks ($10/month)
- Download Evernote, Dropbox, or Box.net and learn how to use them correctly (free)

CREATE A LANDING PAGE

Creating your company's landing page is exciting. It's the first thing you can show people that *this is actually a business.*

Landing pages are easy to build. If you are completely clueless about making landing pages, there are services like LeadPages, LaunchRock, and Unbounce that will do everything for you. You don't have to be good with computers or learn programming. These services will do all the work and hand over a finished landing page that's ready to go.

If you want to be a little more involved, you can set up a blog with WordPress and use it as your landing page. That's still very easy, but will require a bit more setup and work.

It's a common mistake for founders to just slap up a landing page and say, "Okay, we're open for business," and not give people much more than that. A better approach is to think about your ideal customer and what would get them excited. Instead of just giving a bunch of useless information, talk about their problems and how your product can make their life better.

At this stage in the game, you should already know who your ideal customer is. You did that work earlier in the book. You should have an FBI profile of your ideal customer. You should know what their problems are, what their concerns are, what websites they browse to get information. Most importantly, you should know why they have this problem, what their hopes and dreams are, and how the problem you solve stands in their way. Now it's time to use this information. Make your landing page speak to your target customer's hopes, dreams, fears and frustrations.

Instead of creating a bland old landing page that says "Here's my site, give me your email address," offer to give them something for free. And if you don't have anything to give them yet, at least give them something more than just your name. Explain your mission is at least giving them something. Explain why you're trying to do what you're doing.

Use simple, short sentences with plain words. Explain what you're trying to do succinctly. Simple is not easy. Put some care into thinking about what it's like for somebody coming to your landing page for the first time. *What's their story?* Imagine yourself as the target customer coming to your page having never heard about you before. If you plan to put a box that collects an email (and you should), ask yourself, *Why would my target customer* want *to put their email address in there? Why would they be* excited *to give me that information?*

People are bombarded with requests for their personal information all the time. What is it that you can tell your customer that makes it worth their while this time instead of any of the others? What's their burning need and desire? Talk about their hair-on-fire problem. When you think you have come up with some compelling copy, put it online. Then wait. Use your landing page to validate your idea.

A Note about Validation

Early on, I skipped every single one of these steps when starting other companies. I had no separate bank account, no Evernote, and I didn't think about ideal customers. I didn't care why they needed what I was going to build. I just had an idea and thought that was enough. So I would start building it and hope that I would figure out the audience and how to connect with them later.

I never took steps to see if anyone cared. I just thought, *I want that, so it must be something loads of other people want.* Or, *I think that's clever, so I'll build it, and other people will come.*

I would spend weeks or months working on my ideas and side projects. I'd program for a few weeks, get bored, and give up on it. Or, on the rare occasion that I would finish an app and launch it, usually nobody would sign up. Then I'd give up and put it on a shelf with all my other bad ideas. It never occurred to me to use simple validations as a tool before I actually spent time building my ideas.

AppFog was the first time I did things differently, and it was almost entirely by accident.

Heroku is a really cool platform as a service for developers to build apps more easily than ever before. When I discovered it, I was really excited and started moving my own applications over to Heroku. I had lots of Ruby applications, which were perfectly in line with the capabilities of the service; but I also had some PHP applications. Heroku at the time didn't do anything but Ruby.

I desperately wanted to move everything to Heroku, but

I couldn't. Then the little light bulb in my brain switched on and I thought, *There should be a Heroku for PHP*. The name (the terrible name) that came into my head that night was PHP Fog. Ordinarily, I would have started programming after having this thought, but that night was very different from most nights.

Usually when I think I have a great idea, I start building it. I wouldn't even bother talking with my wife. I would usually justify it to myself by thinking that she wouldn't get this anyhow, and I'm just going to do it. On this night, however, I was too tired to write code. Instead, for the first time ever, I just created a landing page. It was an ugly landing page too, just a few sentences and an email box. All it basically said was, "It's like Heroku for PHP." You can still find it at **http://j.mp/phpfog-landing**

Simple. A couple sentences of text and I submitted it to Hacker News (like a Reddit or Digg for programmers), not knowing how it would do. I fell asleep. In the morning, I had eight hundred people signed up. This had never happened to me before. Everything I had experienced up until that point was building something that nobody wanted, launching it, and having nobody sign up for it. All of a sudden, I had eight hundred people that wanted something I hadn't even started building. This was validation. This was traction.

I realized at that moment that validating my idea before building it made so much more sense than the way I had been working before. With validation, I'm assured that all my efforts will be worthwhile. It's how my pregnant wife trusted my claim that people actually wanted what I was creating.

I kept my landing page as is. I didn't promote it or share it anywhere else; I just started coding. Two weeks later, I had a barely working prototype when I checked back in with my email list. It had climbed from eight hundred to four thousand. I didn't have any clue where these people came from. This was true word of mouth. I had unwittingly identified such a hair-on-fire problem that people found me. That day changed my life forever, because I realized for the first time the difference between a hair-on-fire problem and one that wasn't. I realized how significant it was when you have a problem that people know they have, versus ones they don't know they have. AppFog ended up raising ten million dollars and being acquired.

The success of this idea wasn't an accident. I never spent money marketing. I didn't have to because the idea was something people already wanted and were already looking for. The validation was there, and it was my landing page that made it possible.

There are two sides to every coin. Landing pages can be really scary too. A lot of founders are terrified of finding out that nobody wants their great idea. They are scared that nobody will care and nobody will sign up. And the truth is that most of the time nobody will care, and what they think is a great idea is actually a bad idea or just way ahead of its time.

Founders don't want to know that. It's easy to slip into denial and think, *Well, I believe in this idea so much that I don't want to know that people don't care about it as much as I do. I'll just keep building.*

People use this fear to create rat holes. Trust me, I've heard these rat hole excuses so many times. I would say, "Hey, have you created a landing page and tried to get it in front of your ideal customer?"

"Oh, sure, Lucas," they would respond. "I'm going to do

that. It's on my list to do, I just have this, that, the other to do, I just need to work on the product a little more, I don't have the product quite right."

I hear all these excuses. "Oh, yeah, I totally should make a landing page, but I'm just looking for a designer." I had no design on my landing page. None at all. Take a look for yourself: **http://j.mp/phpfog-landing**. I didn't put any work into the design, all I had was words. Just "Like Heroku for PHP," and an email box. That's it.

I didn't make any excuses for myself about why I couldn't do this landing page, and I've heard every excuse in the book. And those excuses come from a place of fear. Fear that nobody will care. You have to get over that fear, because the only thing worse than nobody caring is investing precious time into an idea nobody wants.

But fear can make even a serif vs sans-serif debate seem completely reasonable.

Task Review:

- Landing page: sign up for LandingPages, LaunchRock, or Unbounce; or just use Launch Effect on your WordPress blog
- Save your receipts to Evernote or Dropbox

CREATE A BLOG AND AN EMAIL LIST

I can't tell you how many founders have sat across from me, squirming in their seat as I've asked: "You're doing a great job, you've built a great product, you've even raised funding; but why have you still not created a blog?"

Time after time, I get the same responses: "I need to focus on my product. I don't know how to write. I'm too busy." This brings up one of the interesting things that a lot of founders get wrong, they think that their product is their company and, therefore, it's more important than anything else. This is one of the biggest myths first-time founders believe.

In today's technological age, there is no excuse to not have a blog and an email list.

There is no financial excuse—you can do it for free by going to **blogger.com** or **wordpress.com** and set up your site for free. There's no skill-related excuse—bad writing didn't stop *Fifty Shades of Grey*'s success. There are lots of highly popular blogs with bad writing. There are excuses entrepreneurs tell themselves.

Why is it so important to have an email list? Less than one percent of your Twitter followers will click any given link you post to Twitter. The number can be even smaller for Facebook posts if you don't pay to promote your posts. Posting to Reddit or Digg or Hacker News is a crapshoot that you can't always count on. Compare this to email conversion rates, which can be ten to twenty percent for click-throughs. You need ten to twenty times as many followers on Twitter as you need email newsletter subscribers.

Email is also a much more personal form of communication than social media. It's not like Twitter and Facebook, whose news feeds move so fast it's hard to keep up with everything. Email is one of the only digital touch points that has a high probability of engaging with your audience and creating real relationships.

Why is it so important to have a blog? People begin to recognize you as an authority if you act like an authority and if you sound like an authority. And if you are not already an authority, you can make yourself one is by having created an authoritative blog, or by having people looking to you. In this way, you can establish yourself and your company.

Many people think they can't start a blog until they finish building their product, but that's a terrible excuse. You should build awareness for a product long before you've finished building it. Interact with your industry and interact with your customers. It is not enough to maintain an online presence for only your company. When you have a blog and a mailing list, you can interact with real people. Reach out and use the opportunity to build relationships.

Your product is only one touch point with your customer. You can't build a genuine, deep relationship with your customers with only one touch point. Your blog can be a second touch point. People say, "Okay, I made my website, now I'm going to sit back and wait for people to find it." That doesn't happen. You need to create content that's searchable, and that will make your company discoverable through search engines.

Startups are only as strong as the relationships with their customers. You can't tell customers your story if you're not engaging with them. You can't convert them into fans if they never hear from you. They won't become deep authentic fans unless you let them get to know you personally, not just the company. You can't turn free customers into paid ones if they don't care. You can't just cross your fingers and hope someone will pay someday.

There are so many things you can do to encourage and nurture them into customers. Offering a fourteen-day trial and blindly kicking them out at the end of it is such a wasted opportunity. It's looking at the short term while throwing away the long term. The short term is getting someone to pay in the fourteen-day window. The long term is creating a relationship with a potential customer based on trust and value.

Let's use the example of running a pesticide company. If killing weeds is the only value you offer your customers, then when you fail to sell them pesticides, you have nothing left to talk about. If your mission is to help people grow more crops, then you could be blogging about ten ways to increase yield during a drought or sending email newsletters about new ideas about crop diversification. You have so much more to talk about than just pesticides, and you can create relationships and touch points with potential customers that can offer more opportunities for them to become customers down the road.

If that example seems outlandish, just think again about Nike. When have you seen a Nike commercial telling you to buy their new line of shoes? Nike engages in dialogs about sports and fitness, not about shoes and shoelaces. Apple's famous "'Here's to the Crazy Ones" Think Different' commercial didn't feature a computer, it featured people. And people remember that commercial to this day. How many TV commercials can you remember almost twenty years after they air?

All of the customer touch points that you build should work together as part of a larger strategy connected directly to your mission: your product, your blog, your email list, your social network feed. All touch points should be different forms of engagement of the same mission.

This is how to build fanatical fans that will spread the word about who you are on their own behalf. It's how to grow exponentially. Once you have these kinds of relationships, it's no longer just about your product. That's when you really start to see success. If it's just about your product or platform, you are limiting yourself and your success.

This is very easy advice to ignore, and many founders glaze over it thinking they will get to it "tomorrow." But all of the best companies make this a priority. They use multiple customer touch points to reinforce their message and their mission.

Blog Content

Even when you have a blog and email list, many startups get the content all wrong. They make the same common mistake: all they do is promote their own stuff. The worst thing you can do with a blog is to just announce features and promote yourself.

The best thing you can do with your blog and mailing list is to help and teach people. Give them information that improves their lives.

If you're making fitness enhancement drugs, don't write, "The Ten Best Things About My New Fitness Enhancement Drug." Make your blog about fitness in general, like "Ingenious Ways to Stay Fit When You Travel." Focus on your mission and your core values, rather than your product and features. Write about why you created your product, write about the things that inspire you. The reasons that you created your product are enough to write about.

One of my favorite examples of a company doing this right is Blue Apron. Blue Apron has personally changed my life for the better, and it started out because they give away free recipes on their blog. But the recipes aren't like most recipes, they actually give you the whole meal including side dishes and garnish. It's not just tuna casserole, it's things like roasted poblano and quinoa sopes with avocado, arugula and cherry tomato salad. The sopes and salad go so well together, but I would never have thought of putting them together myself.

After weeks of using different recipes on their website and every dish turning out incredibly, I decided to sign up for their paid service where they ship you all the food in exactly the right proportion to cook Blue Apron recipes every week. You don't need to pay for their service to get the recipes, but once you become a fan, you get drawn into the Blue Apron universe. Their blog doesn't just have free recipes, it also talks about the chefs and restaurants that have inspired them over the years. This is super interesting and draws me deeper into their universe. Their mission is to make home cooking more appealing by sharing great recipes for well-balanced meals, and that's something I completely believe in as well.

How can you turn visitors into fans and supporters of what you do? How can you make it so that when people discover your product or service, they think to themselves: *Where has this been all my life?*

Task Review:

- Blog: Create a WordPress blog either on WP Engine or self-hosted (hosting on **wordpress.com** doesn't allow most plugins or custom themes)
- Mailing list: Sign up for MailChimp, AWeber or Campaign-Monitor and hook it to your landing page and blog using something like SumoMe, OptinMonster, or OptimizePress
- Save your receipts to Evernote or Dropbox

STORYTELLING AND STARTUPS

Storytelling is your job. I used to think the most important thing I could do as a founder was write code. I thought that programming and building the product came before anything else. And for a time, it was true. But as a solo founder, that idea fell apart when I began fundraising. I realized that in order to raise money, I had to put almost all my time into creating and maintaining relationships.

At first, all I could think about was how much time I was spending away from my computer. It felt like I was wasting time, allowing myself to be pulled away from what I was really supposed to be doing, which was writing code. I thought all of that time spent on business development and talking to press to spread the word was a short-term distraction.

When I realized that I couldn't get out of dealing with non-product tasks, I decided to change my perspective on them. I pretended for two weeks that building relationships with customers, VCs, and press was my job, not a distraction. It was like an A/B test. I didn't actually believe it was more important than writing code yet, but I gave myself permission to treat it that way. I gave myself a time box to dedicate myself entirely to building relationships and talking to people. I hired my first employees to take over the product. It was terrifying to hand over the reins.

While treating relationship building as my primary job, it changed everything. I realized that it actually changed the way I approached my conversations. I was no longer short changing people and trying to get them off the phone, but getting to know them and learning their stories. This perspective shift unlocked a lot of success for me, but I see many founders struggle with it. I will ask a pair of early stage founders how many times a week they talk with customers. They will tell me one... at most. They are too busy building the product. I ask them to A/B test for a couple weeks a different set of priorities, and that usually makes all the difference to them as well.

It also changed my conception of what my job truly was. A founder's job, especially the CEO but really any founder's job, is to be a storyteller. You must tell stories to investors, to employees, to customers, to the press, and even to your friends and family. Your job is to be a storyteller. If you do not tell the story, others will invent their own and when you leave others to create your stories, they will inevitably tell the wrong stories.

Maybe you don't think telling stories is important. Maybe you think the product speaks for itself. Denying your role doesn't avoid the responsibility. *You're still a storyteller*, you're just inherently telling bad stories since you're not even trying. So, your job as a founder isn't just to tell stories, it is to tell *good* stories. And that requires practice. Which is where writing comes in.

Even if you're the best storyteller in the world, you can't tell your story once at a time to everyone you meet. It doesn't scale. You'd never reach enough people, it's just not possible. The written word is the most proven way to scale storytelling.

So if you're a founder, especially a CEO, you should treat writing as part of your craft: dedicate time and effort to it, practice, and, most importantly, keep doing it. It doesn't matter how bad you are when you begin. As with anything else, the more you do it the better you will be at it. Writing is one of the most important responsibilities you have, so you have to prioritize it accordingly.

No one can tell stories about your startup, your mission, and what you're doing better than you. It just doesn't work. This cannot be said for most roles within your company. It's entirely possible that another programmer, a contractor, can't code as well as you do, but the code would still work.

You can't hire someone else to tell your story. A contractor cannot understand your target customer and the hair-on-fire problem well enough to come up with your company's core messages. It's not a job you can outsource like HR, bookkeeping, legal, and taxes. You can outsource programming and design but you can't outsource writing and storytelling. Therefore, if you're not regularly writing as a founding CEO, you are avoiding your responsibility. Treat writing and storytelling as a primary part of your job.

Writing is like a muscle. No matter how weak you are right now, you are never too weak to start weight training. Maybe you can only bench press the forty-five-pound bar today, so what? In a couple days you can add five pounds and lift fifty. Then fifty-five pounds a couple days later. Nobody can become Arnold Schwarzenegger overnight. The only proven way to ensure your writing sucks forever is to never train.

Writing became a fundamental part of my role as a founder even after I allowed myself to return to working on the product. I committed myself to writing regularly, and gradually it became less of a grind. It certainly became less scary.

What do you write about if you have no idea where to start? Write about not knowing what to write about. Write about your fears. That's like bench-pressing the empty bar.

When I felt completely lost, I often wrote about it. I never imagined that those posts would be what people responded to most. One of my most popular posts ever was read over a hundred thousand times and drew in thousands of new customers. It was titled: *How We Got Owned by a Few Teenagers (and Why It Will Never Happen Again)*. It started like this: "Hi, I am Lucas Carlson, founder and CEO of PHP Fog and the guy who hasn't slept in almost four days. This is my story."

I was honest, transparent and vulnerable about everything that had happened and what we had done to fix it. And this resonated with people. These are the kinds of things that draw people in and make them a part of your story.

If you're ever lost, one of the best things you can do is write about the process of being lost. Yes, it's scary to put yourself out there by saying, "I'm lost. I don't know what to do. I've got this startup idea and I don't know what to do with it." But that's some of the most engaging content out there. It's what people want to read. It's one of the kinds of stories people are drawn to.

No one wants to read the bullshit most people think they should write: "Announcing my new feature that does x, y, and z. It's twice as fast as every other widget in the world." That story is a terrible bore.

But if you write, "I have this awesome idea and I don't know what to do with it," that's intriguing. That will capture your reader's attention. They will want to follow what happens to see whether you succeed or fail. By simply talking about where you are, you have created a compelling narrative. And please make it personal. Don't act like you are IBM or Microsoft when you are really just a couple guys in a garage. People are far more interested in other people than they are in feature releases.

A company is like a story. The bigger the problem is, the higher your obstacles are, the better the story is. The best stories out there start out with the biggest, most audacious, most awesome problems. And that's how the best companies start out too. Hate your family's business of crime, but finding yourself drawn into it anyhow? That's a big problem that turned into the Godfather. Stuck in an attic hiding from imminent death? Big problem. Anne Frank. Stuck behind enemy lines in World War II, but need to find a soldier anyhow? Big problem. Saving Private Ryan. Stuck on an island with dinosaurs?

The amazing thing about showing vulnerability is that, while your fear is that you're going to sound like an idiot, the truth is you will actually look brave. Your fears say, "You can't write because you're going to sound like an idiot." That's just an excuse. When you acknowledge your fear and do it anyway, you tap into a greater power. If you reveal your humanity to others, you can build a connection and relationship with people.

If you still don't know what to write about, think about yourself five or ten years ago. What would you have wanted to know then that you know now? Write it down, because I assure you that there are people alive right now who are five or ten years younger that could benefit from your point of view. Your writing can seriously help people struggling with issues you are either dealing with now or have dealt with in the past.

If there's one thing that you should not ignore from this book, and if there's one thing you can learn that will radically transform you as a business leader for the rest of your life, it's the importance of writing. If you aren't writing, write. If you don't know what to write, write anyway. Then write more. If you do, you can transform your career and your life.

TALK TO A LAWYER

Finally, find yourself a good lawyer. They don't have to be the most expensive lawyer, but never shop by price for a lawyer. Too often, I've seen founders who think lawyers cost too much money so they will just use templates they find online. That is such a bad idea. I know because I have done it.

There are places where you need to skimp on money and there are places where you cannot possibly afford to skimp on money. This is one of those times.

Yes, good lawyers cost more money than you want to spend, especially in the early stages of building a business. No, you cannot skip hiring one.

Once, I tried to use a cheap lawyer to negotiate a business deal I did with Microsoft. I got tired of paying five hundred dollars per hour to our top-tier firm and thought I could get away with doing this deal with another firm. This firm was known for doing work with other startups in town, so I thought it would be fine at a fraction of the cost.

The cheaper law firm didn't understand the terminology I was using, needed to be handheld the whole time, and still did a bad job in the end. It was frustrating, a waste of my time, and ultimately I had to have my top-tier firm come back and fix things. In my attempts to save money, I ended up paying double.

I was telling this story to a more seasoned entrepreneur, and he explained that not all law firms that charge five hundred dollars per hour are good at what they do, but many law firms charging two hundred dollars per hour don't have the depth of experience that the top firms have.

Choose a lawyer who is very familiar with startups at your

stage and similar to your own. The upsides here are:

- They will be very familiar with your needs and able to advise you much better than a good lawyer with little experience with startups
- They usually allow you to defer payments

Many top-tier startup lawyers with a lot of experience offer to defer payments because they understand that startups are strapped for cash. If they believe in you and what you are doing, they may give you six months or a major funding event (whichever comes first) before you are required to pay their fees.

This way you get the benefits of having a great lawyer without the expense at a time you can't afford it. This gives you the time to try to raise funding. If you can't raise money and the company falls apart before the six months are up, they will write off the debt. It's a loan with the company, not a personal loan with you.

There are ways to be frugal when you need to be frugal. Skipping hiring a lawyer is not one of them. Opting to use legal websites and paperwork templates is fraught with opportunity to shoot yourself in the foot. There are so many different legal terms you will need to pay attention to, and every state has different laws. You could try to figure it all out on your own by doing research online. But it's easy to create a mess for yourself—and you have better things to do with your time.

If the point isn't clear yet, friends don't let friends skimp on their legal representation.

The myriad of logistical tasks you will have to tackle as a

founder, whether they are one-offs or recurring needs, can have a major impact on your startup as it grows. It is essential to incorporate a long-term perspective from the very beginning in order to truly set yourself up for success. Get in the habit of prioritizing the recurring work that is so integral to your role as founder. Learn to focus on the things that are most important instead of falling down logistical rabbit holes. Maintain open, honest communication with your support system and with your customers. Embrace storytelling. Treat your company as your craft. In doing so, you can avoid the pitfalls that trap so many early stage entrepreneurs.

Final Thoughts

As difficult as it is, founding a company is a truly transformative process. It's one of the craziest rides you'll ever take. Sometimes you will feel like you're on top of the world and everything is going your way. Other times the world will be crashing down around you. Building a business can be a very isolating experience. You will feel lonely. You will feel like nobody understands you. But that's not their fault. Few people have had the courage to put everything on the line for an idea. If you are doing it right, you may nearly go bankrupt. And sometimes you might actually go bankrupt. If you do, you will be joining the ranks of Henry Ford, Walt Disney, Donald Trump, P.T. Barnum, and even Abraham Lincoln.

If you are really lucky, you will realize that all the things you were scared of, all the fears that normal people have, are of things that aren't nearly as scary as they once seemed. The things that hold us back are just smoke-and-mirror illusions of an imagined future apocalypse that never arrives. Others will think you brave, but you will know that the boogiemen are just a bunch of shadow puppets on the wall.

It's impossible to emerge on the other end unchanged. And that's the most amazing part—to learn about who you are and grow. It's not just about starting your company, it's about starting a personal journey of exploration.

Starting a company is an act of faith. It's often not a logical one. It rarely ever makes sense. It's always full of risk. The good news is, it's a far less personal downside than it appears at first. It may feel like your career is going to end if you fail. It may feel like you're on the verge of humiliation. It's an internal struggle that feels very real. But by managing your mentality—by taking care of yourself physically, mentally, and emotionally—you can regain control of your thoughts and break free from your fears. You may then realize that, in reality, even failure isn't as scary as you think. You can always get a regular job if you need to.

But that can be hard to remember when things don't make sense (which they won't). The odds are stacked against you. You're more than likely going to fail. How do you have faith that what you're doing matters and that you're actually building toward something greater? How do you actually do it?

The answer certainly doesn't lie in a short-term perspective—*Maybe I can somehow flip this company for one million dollars and retire early.* When times get rough and things don't look like they're going to work out, the thought of being rich will never be enough to keep you going. When it seems like the whole world is against you and it's all falling apart at the seams, you can regain your composure by gaining perspective—a long-term perspective. If you can acknowledge that what you're doing now is part of something bigger—that this is not your last startup—even your failures become valuable experiences that will pave the way for your future endeavors. That's the kind of faith that will get you through the hard times.

This new perspective can help you realize that as hard a time as it might be now, this is teaching you something that's going to be valuable to you later in your career. If your only goal is to get rich, the hard times won't stop, and you will eventually quit when you realize there are faster and easier ways to get rich in life. You can get into real estate or investment banking or become a lawyer.

The struggle is the opportunity. The only way past it is through it. This hard time builds character that you can leverage to your advantage later. This mindset helped me realize the secret to every aspect of a startup: the short-term goal might be to make money, but the long-term goal is building a great relationship with yourself first and then others. Building a great relationship with yourself is commonly called building character. Building great relationships with others is called living.

Long-lasting personal relationships are always more valuable than short-term cash because they have much more leverage and optionality. Always. No matter which area you're working in, whether it's marketing, sales, fundraising, building employee loyalty, building employee enthusiasm, the most valuable thing is relationships. Start the journey by wholly embracing who you are—the good with the bad. Whoever you are, and whatever you really think of yourself when you are all alone staring in the mirror, begin the transformation by telling yourself a new story: "I recognize this as my starting point—the good and the bad. I want to do better today than I did yesterday."

And you will. Over the course of your career as a craftsman

of startups, you will improve your skills, deepen your relationships, and refine your craft. **Keep learning**. Learning about yourself will build your self-confidence, your sense of self and identity, and your own character. Building your relationship with yourself will enable you to build authentic relationships with others. **Keep digging**. Always ask yourself *why*. I still do. Examining the deeper implications of your motivations and decisions will enable you to better understand why you do what you do, which in turn will allow you to do better. **Keep moving**. You're in this for the long haul. Be open to new directions and keep thinking of new ideas. Finding a mission you are passionate about, adhering to your core values *always*, and taking care of your key relationships will ensure that you build a career that you can be proud of.

Most importantly, don't try to take this journey alone. It's a well beaten path with many great guides along the way. Join a community of entrepreneurs, whether that's a local meetup or in a mailing list like **findingsuccessinfailure.com**. Let's do this journey of entrepreneurship together.